Contents

Foreword

THE study of Irish history has changed greatly in recent decades as more evidence becomes available and new insights are provided by the growing number of historians. It is natural, too, that with each generation new questions should be asked about our past. The time has come for a new large-scale history. It is the aim of the Gill History of Ireland to provide this. This series of studies of Irish history, each written by a specialist, is arranged chronologically. But each volume is intended to stand on its own and no attempt has been made to present a uniform history. Diversity of analysis and interpretation is the aim; a group of young historians have tried to express the view of their generation on our past. It is the hope of the editors that the series will help the reader to appreciate in a new way the rich heritage of Ireland's history.

JAMES LYDON, PH.D.
MARGARET MACCURTAIN, PH.D.

For
Uncle Clarke and Aunt Louise,
Lord and Lady MacDermott

'Wisdom is the principal thing; therefore get wisdom: and with all thy getting get understanding.'

Prov. 4:7.

Preface

LIKE so many of the contributors to this series, I also discovered that the time had not yet arrived to write a 'work of reflection' as opposed to one of original research. The imbalance of knowledge made famous by Lecky's *History of Ireland in the eighteenth century* is still present in Irish historiography today. It is to some extent a permanent phenomenon as it is in the nature of events to form peaks of activity, arising from and succeeded by periods of relative quiescence. This situation has been exacerbated by the greater volume and variety of evidence hitherto obtainable for the latter part of the century. However, a considerable amount of material has recently become available for research into the earlier decades and it can be predicted with reasonable confidence that more will be found by the serious investigator. Much of the recently available material used in this study was brought to my attention by Dr A. P. W. Malcomson of the Public Record Office of Northern Ireland, who in addition to other source material showed me a typescript of *Eighteenth century Irish official papers in Great Britain*. Professor G. R. Potter not only drew my attention to the Devonshire MSS. but lent me his transcripts. Quotations from the Devonshire MSS. are by permission of his Grace the Duke of Devonshire and the Trustees of the Chatsworth settled estates to whom I should like to express my thanks. I owe a similar debt to the Earl of Shannon. Dr Noel McLachlan of the University of Melbourne showed me his transcripts of the Wilmot Papers at Derby. I am particularly indebted to these three scholars both for their generosity in sharing their discoveries and for their stimulating discussions upon them.

In preparing this book I have been very conscious of those who might like to read beyond its confines and are, as I have often been, at a distance from large deposits of manuscript sources or adequately stocked libraries. Where I have been able to I have selected quotations and references from the most easily obtainable sources. Surprisingly many printed sources are available, and obscurity of location may add to the curiosity of a document but hardly to its intrinsic merit. In manuscript this study contained approximately twelve pages of detailed references. Restrictions of space have reduced them to one and the same problem has condensed the index to basic proportions. However, the original manuscript, of which this book is partly a derivative, amounted to some 120,000 words and it will be published separately at a later date. In addition to giving footnotes and expanding some of the theories outlined here, it will give a fuller coverage of the social, economic and administrative aspects of Ireland in the eighteenth century.

The Librarians and staff of the libraries of the universities of Sheffield and Melbourne were unfailingly sympathetic to my demands for obscure books. Mrs Pat Holland and Miss Helen Kirk always found time to help me with typing the manuscript. To Professor K. H. D. Haley I am indebted for some enlightening comments on the character of William III. Professor G. R. Potter read the original manuscript and gave me the benefit of his long editorial experience, while Mrs Potter corrected the more exotic variations in my spelling and punctuation—a singular service. Professor Gash continued his guidance to his one-time student and read the original manuscript with his usual promptness and critical care at a very busy time in the academic year. Both sympathised with my problem of selection and neither has seen this version. My sister Margaret Louise not only read the manuscript, but with sisterly candour placed her very extensive and critical knowledge of the history of this period at my disposal. To the understanding of Dr Margaret MacCurtain others have paid tribute and I shall simply add that to me she has shown that true ecumenical charity which 'suffereth long and is kind'.

Edith Mary Johnston
May, 1973

1 Introduction: The Revolution, 1688–92

IN Ireland the eighteenth century was for the élite an age of elegance, and for every section of the community an age of insecurity. This dual inheritance still remains two centuries later. During the eighteenth century ownership of land was the basis of private wealth, social position and political power. By the early decades of the century most of the landed property of the country was in the hands of a small section of the community, who had secured their political supremacy through a policy of religious exclusiveness enforced by the application of a severe penal code. The origins of this situation lay in the seventeenth century, and particularly in the settlement following the Revolution of 1688, when the dynastic and religious implications of the accession of William III and Mary II led to civil war in Ireland.

The settlement at the Restoration in 1660 had confirmed the Irish Protestants in the uneasy possession of the lands which they had acquired as a result of the various confiscations during preceding centuries, particularly those of James I after O'Neill's rebellion, and of Cromwell after the 1641 rebellion. These confiscations had left the dispossessed Catholics with a sense of injustice and a smouldering resentment. Following the Restoration, the long viceroyalty of the 1st Duke of Ormonde had created an unstable tranquillity which had, however, encouraged an unprecedented prosperity, and a growing population was sustained by the expanding economy. Then, as now,

Ireland was an agricultural country, and, with the exception of Dublin, towns were very small. Contemporary opinion, however, considered the city of Dublin to be 'inferior to none in England except *London*; most of the Houses and streets are very regular and modern, and the people as fashionable as anywhere'. Throughout the century Dublin retained its economic, political and social pre-eminence in the life of the country and by the end of the century it had acquired the wide streets and beautiful buildings which made it one of the most elegant cities in Europe.

The fragile political situation changed rapidly with the accession of James II, in 1685, to whom the Catholics looked for support. This hope was encouraged when the king created his long-time associate, Richard Talbot, Earl of Tyrconnell and shortly afterwards sent him over to Ireland as Lord Deputy. 'A tall, proper, handsome man' of rather dubious reputation, Tyrconnell was the younger brother of the Catholic Archbishop of Dublin who had died in 1680 imprisoned during the anti-Catholic agitation created by the fictitious Popish Plot. For the remainder of his life Tyrconnell was the backbone of the Jacobite cause in Ireland, giving his sovereign an unwavering loyalty and an efficient support.

Although the reign of James II began auspiciously, nevertheless, within four years he had completely alienated the English parliament and the majority of his British subjects. Then on 23 December 1688 King James fled to France and the protection of his cousin Louis XIV. In England he was succeeded by his Protestant daughter Mary and her husband William, Prince of Orange, the principal opponent to Louis XIV's plans for territorial aggrandisement in Europe. Shortly afterwards, encouraged by Louis XIV, who wished to distract William's energies and divide his resources, James decided to make a final effort to recover his throne from Ireland where Tyrconnell, refusing to recognise the new sovereigns, had successfully maintained the authority of James II. James arrived in Ireland in March 1689, and by the end of that month Tyrconnell had consolidated his position to such an extent that with the exception of the northern towns of London-derry and Enniskillen all Ireland was in Jacobite hands.

On his arrival James was confronted with three con-current problems: the immediate military necessity of subduing Londonderry and Enniskillen, the urgent need to obtain supplies for military and administrative purposes, and the longer-term necessity of persuading the Irish Catholics, now in the ascendant, to do nothing offensive to the Protestant majority in Great Britain. Confronted with this situation James, contrary to his previous military and administrative reputation, displayed a baffling apathy and a vacillating indecisiveness combined with short flashes of sensible activity. He summoned Parliament on 25 March and it met on 7 May 1689. A lavish exercise of *quo warranto* enquiries ensured Catholic majorities in the corporations which returned M.P.s, – even in Belfast! Only six Protest-ants were returned and these included the two members for Dublin University. On the other hand, although a number of the established episcopate had fled to England, the lords spiritual summoned to the House of Lords were the Anglican bishops who still remained in the country. The family background of one M.P., Sir William Ellis, the Viceroy's secretary, gives an interesting reflection of the political situation: he was a Jacobite official, but he had one brother an Anglican bishop, another a Catholic bishop and a third a Williamite official!

Meanwhile in April 1689 James besieged the fortress and port of Londonderry, cutting the city off from the sea by placing across the river Foyle a boom made of beams studded with iron clamps and held together by a thick rope. The walled city of Londonderry comprised an area of approximately 500 by 300 yards; within it were crammed

3

approximately 30,000 people. However, the besiegers were badly led, inexperienced and ill-equipped. Their only strategy, and one which nearly succeeded, was to subdue the city by famine. Within the city food soon became scarce, indeed as the supply of rats decreased it was reported that one citizen, plumper than the rest, feared the worst and went into hiding! Many died of starvation, but even in face of this, morale remained high and the garrison, commanded by Major Henry Baker and the Reverend George Walker, an Anglican clergyman, refused to consider terms. Finally, on 30 June 1689, the English relief ships, which had been clearly visible to the inhabitants and besiegers alike, broke the boom and sailed into the city. The siege had lasted fifteen weeks and the defending soldiers were so weak that some of them could scarcely stand to their arms. To all the inhabitants victory seemed little short of miraculous. Realising that it was now impossible to capture the city, the Jacobite forces withdrew south and on the following day at Newtown Butler they were severely defeated by the protestant forces based on Enniskillen. Except for some isolated garrisons, by the autumn of 1689 the north was secured for William and Mary, thus providing them with an essential base for next season's campaign.

During the siege parliament had been sitting in Dublin where the basic divergency of objectives between king and parliament speedily led to a mutual disillusionment and James II soon complained that 'he was fallen into the hands of a people who rammed many hard things down his throat'. Although the members returned to this parliament were staunchly Jacobite and almost entirely Catholic, nevertheless, they were determined to erase the 1660 settlement and overturn the existing distribution of land in Ireland before consenting to King James' most pressing need, a grant of supply. James, regarding Ireland as a stepping-stone to the recovery of his English crown, realised that such a policy would be highly offensive to

Protestant England; thus his Catholic parliament placed him in an ever-deepening dilemma as they demanded the repeal of the Acts of Settlement and Explanation. Confident of victory they proceeded to introduce an Act of Attainder, confiscating the lands of almost every Protestant landholder in the kingdom. Other legislation removed any religious basis for civil disabilities and established the exclusive right of each denomination to the tithes of its members. Finally parliament asserted its long-debated right to be the exclusive legislative and ultimate judicial authority for Ireland, and only royal opposition prevented the repeal of Poynings' Law.

The implementation of this policy depended upon military victory. Its discussion, during the siege of Londonderry, inevitably hardened the resistance of the already terrified protestants. The subsequent defeat of the Catholic forces made the declared policy of the Jacobite parliament a convenient justification for a Protestant retaliation; a retaliation which bore a direct ratio to the fears that had been confirmed. While parliament was debating its grievances and formulating its future policy, the financial situation deteriorated rapidly as the war disrupted the economy of the country. James was forced to debase the currency, issuing the notorious 'brass money' which people refused to accept at its face value thereby creating further chaos in the shattered economy of the country.

Following the siege of Londonderry William III sent troops to the north of Ireland under the command of his eighty-two year old marshal, the Huguenot Duke of Schomberg, a man of vast experience, who, we are told, 'knew men and things beyond most in his time' and 'commanded Respect from Men of all Qualities and stations'. On his arrival in August 1689, Schomberg spent the remainder of the campaigning season consolidating William's hold on the North before going into winter quarters at Lisburn. Never very enthusiastic, in view of William's systematic preparations, James II began to lose heart and accepted Louis XIV's offer of French troops in exchange for Irish. The Irish troops which went to France, both at this time and after the Treaty of Limerick, formed the nucleus of the Irish Brigade whose three famous regiments, Mountcashel's, O'Brien's and Dillon's fought with such distinction in France's wars of the eighteenth century. In return 7,000 French troops under the command of the erratic duc de Lauzun arrived in Ireland during the following March. James II and de Lauzun were still in Dublin when William III landed at Carrickfergus on 14 June 1690.

Much has been written about the curiously enigmatic character of the Dutch king of England who was to occupy so indelible a place in the history of the country in which he campaigned for a few short months in 1690, and where he won one of his few decisive victories. Outwardly an austere Calvinist, inured to hardship and reverses, this icy exterior concealed a man who in private life was a loyal and sympathetic friend and an affectionate husband. A formidably efficient organiser, in his vast schemes for the destinies of Europe, Ireland, like England, was only a stepping-stone, albeit in the summer of 1690 an all-important one. It is perhaps a supreme irony that neither of the monarchs involved in this decisive war considered the fate of the country over which they were fighting as a primary cause of their struggle, nor its destiny of paramount importance, except as a means to an end.

On William's arrival, James moved north and finally decided to meet William in the valley of the Boyne at a point about thirty miles north of Dublin and five miles west of Drogheda. Winding through a landscape of rolling drumlin-hills, the Boyne was described by one participant in the battle as 'a great and rapid river, and whatever it has been formerly, it will be famous in succeeding Ages from this Action'. Certainly it was the best strategic point from which to defend the capital from an attack from Ulster.

The first or (depending upon the old or new style calendar) the twelfth of July 1690, dawned a clear and beautiful summer day 'as if the sun itself had a Mind to see what would happen'. Taking advantage of the long daylight troops began to move about 6 a.m. James had the advantage of position, William in the number and experience of his troops, particularly in his Dutch guards of whose prowess he was exceedingly proud and for whose welfare he was particularly concerned, being heard to murmur at the height of the battle, 'my poor guards, my poor guards'.

Ill-trained and ill-led, the Irish infantry were unable to resist the pressure of the guards' frontal attack. The strength of the Irish army lay in its cavalry which made a brave stand under Berwick, Hamilton and Tyrconnell, and when the fight was over William counted among his dead the octogenarian Duke of Schomberg and Walker, the defender of Londonderry. During the afternoon James 'when he saw how things were like to go marched off to Duleek, and from thence towards Dublin' where he advised the citizens 'that they should make the best terms for themselves that they could, and not to burn or injure the town'. Then, accompanied by about a dozen followers, he fled to France, leaving William master of Ireland east of the river Shannon.

It was now William's turn to face the dilemma posed by the divergence between his own views and those of his subjects, for William, regarding the war primarily in its European context, was not unwilling to offer the Jacobites generous terms for a speedy conclusion of hostilities which would release his troops for the defence of the Netherlands and a unified stand against Louis XIV. The English and Irish parliaments, however, were anxious to reduce the expenses of the war through the sale of Jacobite estates. In addition, the Irish Protestants, still smarting from the Act of Attainder, wanted revenge and the fruits of their recent victory. Under these pressures William demanded what amounted to an unconditional surrender from the Jacobites, specifically offering them no security of property. This stiffened the Jacobite opposition, who now had nothing to lose and possibly better terms to gain.

The line of the Shannon was held by the fortress of Athlone and the city of Limerick to which Tyrconnell, encouraged by Louis XIV to continue the struggle, now retreated. Hoping to complete the war before the end of the campaigning season, William marched on Limerick. His hopes were disappointed by the guerilla activities of Patrick Sarsfield. Moving more slowly than the main body of the army, William's heavy siege-train was encamped some seven miles distant from the main camp at a place called Ballyneety. Here disaster struck, for 'thinking themselves at home so nigh the Camp . . . they turn'd most of their horses out to Grass . . . and the guard they left was but a very slender one, the rest most of them going to sleep; but some of them awoke in the next world; for *Sarsfield* all that day lurked among the mountains . . . he fell in among them before they were aware . . . [and] blew up all with an astonishing noise . . . This news', the reporter concludes, 'was very unwelcome to everybody in the Camp.'

Patrick Sarsfield, whom James II created Earl of Lucan, was described by that monarch's illegitimate son, the Duke of Berwick, as 'a man of an amazing stature, utterly void of sense, very good natured and very brave'. Educated at a French military academy, he was killed in Louis XIV's service at Landen in 1693. The attraction of his personality, the Ballyneety incident and his subsequent behaviour during the siege and the negotiations for the Treaty of Limerick gave him an enduring and legendary fame among his countrymen. Meanwhile, encouraged by Sarsfield's triumph, the Irish rallied and William failed to capture Limerick during the few weeks which remained of the campaigning season of 1690. At the end of August, William himself left Ireland, appointing his Dutch general,

Baron de Ginkel, afterwards Earl of Athlone, to command his forces.

Despite their initial success in holding Limerick, fatal divisions soon appeared among the Irish command, where differences of personality began to aggravate the differences inherent in the objectives of James II, Louis XIV and the Jacobite Irish. Tyrconnell, as James II's Lord Deputy, commanded at Limerick. In January the French commander, the duc de Lauzun, whose curious career had already included an attempt to ally himself to the French royal family through a marriage to Louis XIV's cousin, Mlle de Montpensier, the richest heiress in France, was recalled and replaced by the Marquis de St Ruth. According to the duc de Saint Simon and Madame de Sévigné the career of St Ruth was also strange. A remarkably ugly man of comparatively simple origins he had married the widow of the Maréchal de la Meilleraye. He became a confirmed wife-beater. As he did not heed the king's reproof, he was posted first to Guyenne and then to Ireland. Soon Tyrconnell, St Ruth and Sarsfield were divided by mutual dislike and jealousies, while adequate French supplies failed to materialise despite Louis XIV's encouragement to continue the war.

Ginkel opened the 1691 campaign by marching on Athlone, a strong fortress divided by the river Shannon. On 30 June, after a sharp struggle and despite the proximity of St Ruth, Ginkel was master of both sections of the city. St Ruth had considered the fortress impregnable, and discovering his mistake, he 'was resolved to retrieve his loss or Dye, since he could not be answerable to his Master that imployed him for what had already happened: and therefore he used all means possible to strengthen his Army and find out a convenient place to try his Fortune in'. Fortune, however, did not favour St Ruth when he met Ginkel at Aughrim on 12 July 1691. Before the battle some attempt appears to have been made to convince the untrained Irish soldiers in St Ruth's army that they were fighting a holy crusade. At the beginning of the battle the advantage lay with neither side until a chance cannon shot removed St Ruth's head. Shaken by this event his forces wavered and fled. A terrible carnage then ensued, and although the Boyne was the decisive battle of the war, Aughrim proved the more costly in terms of human life and enduring misery.

Following the battle of Aughrim Galway surrendered on 21 July, leaving Limerick as the only remaining Jacobite stronghold, and here on 14 August Tyrconnell suddenly died of apoplexy following a dinner-party. The Irish command now devolved on Sarsfield, who, when the imminently promised French reinforcements did not arrive, considering the situation to be hopeless decided to make the best terms that he could both for the army and for its Jacobite supporters, relying on Ginkel's wish to conclude the campaign as soon as possible. Both Ginkel and Sarsfield were anxious to arrive at a just settlement, which would resolve the Irish war and leave them at liberty to continue the European struggle abroad, and to this end they concluded the Treaty of Limerick on 3 October 1691. Few documents have been the subject of more debate and recrimination, possibly because of the underlying division of interests between those who formed it, those upon whom it was imposed and those who were required to ratify it.

The Treaty contained two sets of articles, civil and military. The military articles, arranging for the surrender of the city, the release of prisoners and the transport abroad of such Jacobite forces as wished to leave Ireland, were faithfully fulfilled. Two days after the articles had been signed the French reinforcements arrived and, although encouraged to remain, Sarsfield with some 5,000 troops left on the returning French ships. A further 6,000 men were subsequently transported to France by ships of the British fleet then at war with France. It has been estimated that approximately 12,000 Irish troops were added to the forces of Louis XIV at this time. They augmented the Irish troops already in France and, as the regiments of the Irish Brigade, remained a distinguished part of the French army until the French Revolution reorganised the armies of the *ancien régime* to which they had belonged. Fighting in the red-coats of the British army, their existence and their exploits gave a credibility to the Stuart cause long after it had any political validity. Recruitment for these regiments continued throughout most of the eighteenth century and, although it is difficult to assess the consequences precisely, the effect of this continuous drain on Catholic Irish society must have been very considerable. However, once they had been settled, the military articles proved the most satisfactory part of the negotiations, and future disputes were confined to the confirmation and interpretation of the civil articles.

The civil articles were framed with three principal objectives: firstly to allow the Roman Catholics such a degree of toleration 'as may preserve them from any Disturbance, upon Account of their said religion', and the minimum definition of this was to be 'such Privileges in the exercise of their religion as are consistent with the Laws of Ireland; or as they did enjoy during the Reign of King Charles the II'. Unfortunately this was a very vague statement; the Elizabethan anti-Catholic legislation was on the statute book and although Catholics had generally not been interfered with during the reign of Charles II, there had been occasional anti-Catholic outbursts as during the Popish Plot when the Catholic Archbishop of Armagh had been executed at Tyburn. The second objective was to guarantee security of life and property to Jacobite officers and soldiers who, remaining in Ireland, wished to accept the new government and to acquire a similar immunity for the merchants and inhabitants of Limerick and other Jacobite strongholds still in Irish possession at the time of the Treaty.

The original articles had an additional clause offering a special reassurance to Jacobite forces in counties Limerick, Clare, Kerry, Cork and Mayo 'and all such as are under their protection in the said counties'. This last phrase was the famous 'missing clause' accidentally left out of the final copy of the Treaty. All the evidence indicated that it was left out by a clerical error, and William and Mary, despite the opposition of the English Privy Council, issued letters patent rectifying the omission. Nevertheless, it continued to be a matter for debate. The third important condition of the civil articles was that 'the oath to be administered to such Roman Catholics as submit to their Majesties' Government, shall be the Oath abovesaid (the simple Oath of Allegiance), and no other'.

Magnanimous in victory and preoccupied abroad, William III would have been glad to grant the terms of the Treaty in the spirit in which it had been framed, and to obtain the confirmation of its articles from the Irish parliament at an early date. However, William's viceroys, particularly Lord Sydney in 1692, found the Protestant Irish parliament as self-interested and recalcitrant as James II had found the Catholic Irish parliament in 1689. For political reasons, the bill confirming the Treaty was not introduced until 1697 and then in a very mutilated form. No reference was made to the Catholics enjoying the exercise of their religion as they had done during the reign of Charles II, there was no mention of the oath, and although the privileges granted to those under arms at the time of the Treaty were confirmed, the 'missing clause' remained in abeyance. However, many of the individual claims for the restoration of estates had in fact already been heard and allowed by the Irish Privy Council, which by the end of 1694 had heard 491 claims and allowed 483 of them. By the closing date in 1699 nearly 1,200 claims had been heard and almost all granted. Among those allowed were claims from most of the leading Jacobite families including

Lords Antrim, Clanricarde, Dillon, Dunboyne, Dunsany, Fitzwilliam of Merrion, Kingsland, Westmeath, Louth, Mountgarrett, Gormanston and Iveagh. Nevertheless, this concession was limited to those who were undefeated at the time of the Treaty, and excluded those who had previously surrendered during the course of the campaign.

From the way in which these claims were allowed, the Treaty of Limerick did succeed in circumscribing the extent of the confiscations. Ultimately even the 'missing clause' was not without effect as, although it was left out of the confirmation, the Irish Lord Chancellor suggested that the king could make it effective simply by failing to prosecute Catholic landowners in those areas, and there is some evidence that this suggestion was put into practice especially in the counties most affected, Clare and Mayo. As a result of this final confiscation the Catholics lost about one-third of the lands which they had held during the reign of James II. Some indication of the extent and speed of the land confiscations in the latter part of the seventeenth century can be grasped from the fact that in 1640 the Catholics possessed nearly 60 per cent of the land of Ireland; by 1688 their holdings had been reduced to 22 per cent and after the Williamite confiscations to 14 per cent. This slender possession was to be still further eroded by the imposition and operation of a religious penal code which was against not only the Treaty of Limerick but also any hope of an enduring peace in Ireland.

Historians have tended to concentrate on the political and religious aspects of the eighteenth century and restrictions of space and more importantly of knowledge have ensured that this short study will do likewise. Nevertheless, Irish life in the eighteenth century was not only shaped by the political and social effects of the changes consolidated by the Williamite confiscations and the Penal Laws, but also by the economic and social consequences of the unprecedented rise in population on an agrarian economy, which

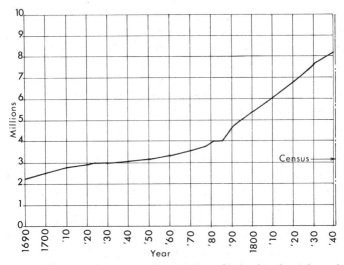

Graph showing the estimated population of Ireland in the eighteenth century indicating the rapid increase which marked its close and continued until the Famine. (From the figures given in K. H. Connell, The Population of Ireland, 1750–1845, p.25)

did not possess the natural resources to enable it to absorb its increasing population into an industrial society. The population of Ireland in the eighteenth century has been the cause of much study and more speculation. It is impossible to assess it precisely and the estimate of Professor Connell, illustrated on the accompanying graph, is possibly the closest approximation. These figures, which are probably conservative, estimate that the population in 1700 was approximately $2\frac{1}{2}$ million and that by 1800 it had risen to approximately $5\frac{1}{2}$ million. The rise was comparatively steady until the middle of the 1780s, when a rapid upsurge began and continued until the great famine of the mid-nineteenth century. Then it declined rapidly and today the population of Ireland is approximately what it was in the mid-eighteenth century.

It is difficult to estimate the individual impact of the

numerous interrelated factors which contributed to this astonishing phenomenon. For example, was the increasing dominance of the potato in the national diet, coupled with the development of a more prolific variety, a cause or effect? Was fertility increasing due to earlier marriages, better health or for some other reason? Were the famines which had recurred with such devastating consequences in the earlier part of the century less severe in its latter half? Was there a hiatus in emigration either to North America or to the continent following the American war and subsequent European disturbances? Was the national health improving because of inoculation and improved medical care? Probably all of these and other factors contributed to some degree, but lack of statistical evidence makes direct attribution impossible. Possibly the two most important factors were the adequate diet provided by the increasing cultivation of the potato, without which the growth in population could not have been sustained, and the increasing fertility resulting from earlier marriages. Famines, which were distressingly common during the earlier years of the century, do not appear to have been so severe after the great famine of 1740–1. Nevertheless, although conditions were improving throughout the century, the depressing hopelessness of life for the majority made early marriages not disadvantageous, for a large family offered the only security against old age and destitution in a country which had no poor law and virtually no provision for any form of social welfare.

The Protestant ascendancy were not insensitive to the plight of the poor around them. The liberal and humanitarian ideas which gradually gained impetus in the second half of the eighteenth century found a practical expression in the number of Dublin hospitals founded during this period, and a theoretical one in pamphlets like that published by Dr Woodward, Bishop of Cloyne, in 1768, entitled 'An Argument in Support of the Right of the Poor in

Ireland to a National Provision'. However, the arrangement of social aid is always a difficult and delicate task both
practically and psychologically, and many well-intentioned
schemes foundered through inadequate knowledge and
inefficient organisation. For instance, the Foundling Hospital for the preservation (and proselytisation) of unwanted
infants was, despite the good intentions of its founders, one
of the most horrific social experiments ever undertaken in
Ireland. Many infants were abandoned in the harsh social
climate of the eighteenth century, and the hospital accepted
all the deserted children offered to it. Unfortunately this did
little to improve their situation, as the mortality rates of children entered on the hospital's records remained excessively
high. During the years 1784 to 1796, of 25,352 children
17,253 died – not all inside the hospital, as some were nursed
outside. The Irish House of Commons was shocked at 'facts
which carry a complexion of more than savage cruelty'.
The hospital was reorganised, and for a time the mortality
rate fell, but by 1826 the situation had deteriorated once
more. This time the hospital was finally closed, when a
further report, equally horrifying in detail, concluded that it
was 'evidently the design of Providence that the infancy of
children should be superintended by their parents, and that
a great departure from this principle . . . will be attended by
circumstances of an untoward and perplexing nature'. Fear
as well as indolence lay behind the doctrine of *laissez-faire*,
especially when the fragile nature of society was underlined
by the collapse of well-intentioned experiments. Nevertheless, it was from these failures that better and more effective
methods of ameliorating social distress eventually emerged.

2 Religion in the Eighteenth Century

THE seventeenth century's recurring waves of rebellion and revolution had gradually eroded the political and economic position of the Catholic majority. The years following the Treaty of Limerick witnessed its virtual political annihilation until in 1739 a pamphleteer could declare, 'there are not twenty Papists in Ireland who possess each £1,000 a year in land and the estates belonging to others of a less yearly value are proportionally few': an opinion which was confirmed by Lord Lieutenant Townshend in 1772 when he wrote to the Secretary of State in London, 'the laws against popery have so far operated that at this day there is no popish family remaining of any great weight from landed property'. These 'laws against popery' are collectively known as the Penal Code, and Edmund Burke, whose maternal grandfather was among those whose claims were allowed under the terms of the Treaty of Limerick, described them as a 'machine as well fitted for the oppression, impoverishment and degradation of a people, and the debasement in them of human nature itself as ever proceeded from the perverted ingenuity of man'. The extent and the implication of so devastating a system inflicted on so great a majority of the population, is undoubtedly central to any consideration of Ireland in the eighteenth century, and it requires examination both for what it actually was and for what subsequent generations have believed it to be.

The Penal Code was a system of laws with a religious

bias aimed mainly against Roman Catholics, but also to an extent against all who were not members of 'the Church of Ireland as by law established'. The enactments began shortly after the Treaty of Limerick and reached their climax during the reign of Queen Anne. Although they continued into the reigns of the early Hanoverians, as the Protestant succession became secure, particularly after the failure of the '45 rebellion, they gradually lost their momentum. Thus, the years in which the Penal Laws were most harshly enforced coincide with the era in which Jacobitism was, or was felt to be, a genuine force in British politics. Within six years of the accession of George III, James Edward Stuart died, and this further encouraged the erosion of the Penal Code which had already started about a decade earlier. The Code's penalties were first gradually ignored, then legally abolished in a series of piecemeal repeals starting in 1778 and culminating in the Catholic Emancipation Act of 1829, which brought a final measure of relief to all Catholics in the by then United Kingdom of Great Britain and Ireland. Some months previously a similar relief had been granted to all protestant non-conformists, who had also been second-class citizens in both countries, and who had automatically benefited from the Catholic agitation. Fundamentally the success of the Penal Code was a tribute to the sincerity with which both Catholic and protestant non-conformists held their religious convictions: it could not have operated otherwise.

The purpose of the Penal Laws was principally to manipulate a religious situation, which approximated to a racial division, in order to establish a social, political and, to a considerable extent, an economic monopoly in the hands of a narrow group. The members of this group differed from the overwhelming majority of the population in being usually the descendants of English settlers and invariably members of the Anglican Church of Ireland. 'The Penal Code', declared Grattan, who, at the end of the century saw in it the great barrier to national unity, 'was the shell in which Protestant power had been hatched'. Its conception and the consequences of its birth are perhaps more obvious than the reasons for its nurture, which lie not only in the greed and fear of the Protestant ascendancy, but also in the home and foreign policy of England in the early eighteenth century.

Except for a few years during the reign of Anne, when the High Church party in England shared the ascendancy's policy of religious exclusiveness, the British administration had reluctantly consented to the Irish parliament's penal policy in order to secure the tranquillity of Irish government and the safe passage of the Money Bills. By temporising to meet what were usually the necessities of the moment, they became increasingly bound to the self-centred blackmail of a narrow class who were in their turn both fearful and isolated, for as the House of Commons told Queen Anne in 1709, 'the tithes of more than half the estates now belonging to the Protestants depend upon the forfeitures in the last two rebellions in which the generality of the Irish were engaged'.

It should perhaps be stated that the word 'Protestant' in eighteenth-century Ireland usually refers to Anglican and excludes the non-conforming protestant denominations. The operation of the Penal Code created on a religious basis what was in many ways a typical colonial situation, and one which contemporaries certainly regarded as such. Lord Chesterfield, Lord Lieutenant 1745-6, considered that 'the poor people of Ireland are used worse than negroes'. During the eighteenth century colour and slavery were not the only badges and methods by which a small minority kept a large majority in subjection.

To the British administration Ireland's international position was certainly of equal, and probably in the early years of the century of greater, importance than the clamour of the emerging ascendancy for vengeance, security and later parliamentary independence. The Hanoverian succession was for contemporaries far from the foregone conclusion it appears in retrospect, and the whole issue with all its implications remained a central element in the political scene until after the defeat of Charles Edward Stuart at Culloden in 1746. At the beginning of the eighteenth century the struggle for dominance between England and France had barely commenced and, considering the many vicissitudes of the wars of the century, it is not surprising that the early eighteenth-century politicians did not confidently predict our knowledge of the outcome.

From the time of Tacitus onwards the implication of the geographical position of Ireland has been a source of historical and political speculation. The view of eighteenth-century Englishmen, expressed in 1784, was that 'Ireland is too great to be unconnected with us, and too near us to be dependent on a foreign state, and too little to be independent'. It was this position which had encouraged Louis XIV's interference in the war between James II and William III. The Irish troops which had fought against William at the Boyne, Aughrim and Limerick opposed him again in the European theatres of the War of the League of Augsburg; Sarsfield died in 1693 fighting for France, and during the following year the founder of the Irish Brigade, Justin MacCarthy, Lord Mountcashel, died as a result of wounds similarly sustained in the service of Louis XIV.

England was at war with France between 1689 and 1697, the war of the League of Augsburg, and again between 1702 and 1713, the war of the Grand Alliance. The English succession question was an element in both these wars, and it was these years that saw the enactment of the worst aspects of the Penal Code. The reign of William III saw bills to prevent Catholics from educating their children abroad, to disarm Catholics and to banish the Catholic hierarchy and regular clergy; Queen Anne's parliament not only passed further Acts against the clergy but also the

4 Act 'to prevent the further growth of with its 1709 sequel was the harshest of all s, – 1704 was the year of Blenheim and ⊔et. Not only in the wars of William III, ⊔nne, but throughout the eighteenth century ⊔f France had a brigade of Irish troops which were ⊔ually being recruited from Ireland and used to fight ⊔gainst England often, as at Dettingen in 1744, with considerable success.

In the seventeenth century it was felt that a man's religion was a guide to his political attitudes; hence the famous phrase in the 1689 English Bill of Rights that 'it is inconsistent with the safety and welfare of this Protestant kingdom to be governed by a Popish Prince'. Only four years earlier, in the interests of religious uniformity, Louis XIV had revoked the Edict of Nantes, and the ensuing expulsion of large numbers of highly skilled Huguenot refugees greatly benefited not only England and Ireland but also most of protestant Europe. Toleration was not a widely known or accepted concept in the seventeenth century.

In March 1702 William III died in Kensington Palace, his frail body worn out by the great schemes which consumed it, his mind with reluctant fortitude relinquishing them to his successors. Six months earlier the exiled James II had predeceased him. At the time of his death it was already clear that neither William III nor his successor, the Princess Anne, would leave direct heirs. The Act of Settlement had, therefore, decreed that, under these circumstances, the throne would pass to the Electress Sophia of Hanover, a grand-daughter of James I, and her heirs 'being Protestants'. Nevertheless, the future inevitably had an element of indecisiveness, which encouraged both Louis XIV and the Pope to recognise the twelve-year-old James Edward Stuart as James III. This recognition had both immediate and long-term consequences: the enraged

English parliament consolidated William's Grand Al[...]
against the French king, while until the death of Ja[...]
Edward in 1766 successive Popes almost invaria[...]
accepted his nominations to the Irish Catholic hierarch[...]
Although there is every indication that this privilege was
well and carefully used for the benefit of the Church, the
paradox implicit in the situation inevitably placed the
ordinary Irish Catholic in an undeservedly ambiguous
position. For example it resulted in the banned but influential international orders of the Dominicans and Fran-
ciscans being active as well as passive supporters of the
Stuarts. In 1727 the Franciscan Provincial, Francis Stuart,
used his influence against Lord Devlin's proposal for a loyal
address from the Irish Catholics to George II on his accession. This apparent conflict of loyalty had been further
emphasised by the exodus of the Irish Catholic aristocracy
following the Treaty of Limerick, which left the Irish
peasantry without their natural leaders.

Throughout the eighteenth century the links of Catholic
Ireland with the continent were extremely close and affected
a wide spectrum of Irish life: commercial links through
the Irish merchant houses established at ports such as Nantes
and Bordeaux; military links through the Irish Brigade,
particularly the crack regiments continually recruited from
Ireland which fought with distinction in the service of
France throughout the century, although other Irishmen
could be found in the armies of Spain, Sardinia and Austria;
finally there were educational links as virtually all the Irish
clergy and the sons of the more prosperous laity were
educated at one or other of the Irish colleges scattered
throughout Europe. The largest and most frequented of
these colleges were those established in France where the
colleges at Nantes and Paris alone could accommodate as
many as one hundred students. All except two of these
colleges were already in existence before 1690 and they
flourished until the 1770s, when they suffered considerably

by the suppression of the Society of Jesus. Their downfall was completed by the French Revolution. However, by that time virtually all of the Penal Code had been repealed, and, during the 1790s, with government encouragement, Catholic Colleges were established in Ireland where in 1793 St Patrick's College was founded at Carlow and two years later St Patrick's College, Maynooth.

Many of those educated abroad did not return, and probably could not have been absorbed had they done so. In 1748 there were 39 Irish priests working in the Gironde alone, and the parish of Boyentran had between 1696 and 1766 a continuous succession of Irish priests. This area was particularly popular because of the Irish Colleges at Nantes, Poitiers and Bordeaux and the Irish merchants in the two ports. Some Irish priests rose to very high office indeed. Possibly the most eminent Irish cleric was a member of the aristocratic Dillon family: Arthur Richard Dillon entered the Catholic Church in France to become successively Bishop of Evreux in 1753, Archbishop of Toulouse in 1758 and Archbishop of Narbonne in 1763, Commander of the Order of the Holy Ghost, Primate of the Gauls, President of the State of Languedoc; he was also twice a member of the Assembly of Notables and twice President of the clergy of France. He died in London in 1806. His nephew, General Arthur Dillon, who had fought the British in America and the West Indies and led the family regiment in the Irish Brigade, was among those who perished in the reign of terror. He retained to the end a reputation for politeness and gallantry, as when he arrived at the scaffold a lady, who was in the same predicament, requested that he should precede her and he smilingly replied, 'Anything to oblige a lady'!

The old Irish connection was with the France of the monarchy and the *ancien régime,* and it perished with it. The last Colonel of the Irish Brigade was General Daniel, Count O'Connell, who owing to the circumstances of his day was both a French royalist general and a British colonel. In 1794 the Irish Brigade accepted George III's invitation to join the British army, and a fourth regiment was created and given to O'Connell. Thus while the United Irishmen were negotiating with revolutionary France, the descendants of the Jacobites, in the interests of the Bourbon Louis XVIII, were serving the Hanoverian George III. In June 1789 O'Connell had written to his brother Maurice O'Connell, 'I have made all possible enquiries for the properest place to send our nephews Dan and Maurice of Carhen, and from the informations I collected have room to conclude St Omer's is the most suitable . . . where I shall previously make it my business to ensure their admittance, I presume they may cost you about £40 or £50 a year each.' This education in France, at the beginning of the Revolution, possibly encouraged O'Connell's subsequent preference for constitutional, rather than violent, political methods in the struggle for Catholic Emancipation. Count O'Connell witnessed his nephew's triumph before he died in his ninetieth year in 1833.

Many distinguished scholars of Irish origin were to be found not only in the Irish Colleges but in several of the universities of Catholic Europe from Flanders to Italy, Spain and Portugal. It is difficult not to sympathise with Daniel O'Reilly, who, when president of the Irish College at Antwerp, learnt in 1748 of his elevation to the bishopric of Clogher and remarked that he would prefer a benefice worth 300 florins in the Netherlands. However, he duly expressed his gratitude to 'James III' for the honour which had been bestowed on him and departed for Ireland. The bishopric to which Bishop O'Reilly so reluctantly came had in fact little to recommend it. It was in predominantly Presbyterian Ulster and the majority of the inhabitants had all the Genevan fear and horror of the Roman Church. They were little disposed to regard their Catholic neighbours as fellow victims of the penal system. The local author Carleton has recorded a vivid description of Bishop O'Reilly's diocese as it was in the early nineteenth century. 'There was nothing in existence for the Catholics for the worship of God', he writes, 'except the mere altar covered with a little open roof to protect the priest from rain, which it was incapable of doing. The altar was about two feet in depth and the open shed which covered it not more than three . . . There was always a little plot of green sward allowed to be annexed to the altar on which the congregation could kneel, as neither man nor woman could kneel on a wet sward, through which the moist yellow clay was oozing, without soiling or disfiguring their dress or catching cold from the damp . . . during the winter months the Worship of God was in one sense a very trying ceremony.'

Throughout the eighteenth century both clergy and people were extremely poor. From the examination of Nicholas Sweetman, who became Bishop of Ferns in the mid-1740s, it appears that on an average a parish priest received £30–£35 a year and that some priests received corn and other small gifts from their parishioners either as part of or in addition to their remuneration. At the end of the century the question arose of some form of government support for the Catholic clergy. In 1799 Archbishop Troy considered 'that a provision through government for the Roman clergy of this kingdom, competent and secured ought to be thankfully accepted'. However, the opposing view was expressed to the French traveller de Tocqueville by a poor parish priest in the West of Ireland, who explained that: 'the people give the fruit of their labours liberally to me and I give them my time, my care and my entire soul . . . Between us there is a ceaseless exchange of feelings of affection. The day I received government money, the people would no longer regard me as their own.'

It is difficult not to conclude that the mass of the Catholic people of Ireland, left leaderless by the partially voluntary

25

exile of their natural leaders, the Catholic aristocracy who fled to France after the Jacobite Wars, drawn, by the dual loyalty of the ecclesiastical hierarchy to the Pope and the exiled House of Stuart, into the maelstrom of the European wars of the eighteenth century, were the victims of the policies of their own leaders as well as of the fear and avarice of the Protestant Irish parliament. Certainly the prominent Catholics who remained were too weak and too disheartened to form anything like a solid group to oppose the aggrandisement of the Anglican ascendancy. Frequently to conform if their conscience would allow, and salvage what they could from the holocaust must have seemed to many Catholics the only possible policy: ''Tis sad for me', wrote one in such a dilemma, 'to cleave to Calvin or perverse Luther but the weeping of my children, the spoiling them of flocks and lands brought streaming floods from my eyes . . .' Members of Catholic families, like John Fitzgibbon, father of the Earl of Clare, conformed in order to enter upon a professional career. In 1728 Archbishop Boulter complained that: 'the practice of the law from top to bottom is at present mostly in the hands of new converts, who gave no further security of this account than producing a certificate of their having received the sacrament in the Church of England or Ireland – which several of them, who were Papists at London, obtained on the road hither – and demand to be admitted barristers by virtue of it on their arrival, and several of them have Popish wives, and mass said in their houses, and breed up their children Papists. Things are at present so bad with us, that, if about six should be removed from the bar to the bench here, there will not be a barrister of note left that is not a convert.'

Anti-Catholic laws had been in existence from the sixteenth century, for Henry VIII and Elizabeth I had endeavoured to extend the reformation to Ireland. However, although the penal legislation existed, its application had proved difficult, and the unsettled state of the country during the seventeenth century had made its enforcement spasmodic and largely ineffective. For example the 1560 Act of Uniformity which required attendance at the state church on Sundays or the payment of a shilling fine had fallen into complete disuse by the end of the seventeenth century. No attempt was made to operate this statute during the eighteenth century, although it was not actually repealed until 1793. During the seventeenth century there had been occasional outbreaks of anti-Catholic feeling, for instance during the Popish Plot scare in the reign of Charles II, but in general the Catholics had been allowed to exercise their religion with little interference, and it was this practical situation rather than the theoretical one that the Treaty of Limerick had sought to preserve.

The Penal Code of the late seventeenth and early eighteenth centuries comprised laws imposing civil disabilities on the one hand, and religious restrictions on the other. Although many of the laws contained elements of both, it is possibly simpler to consider these two aspects separately. The civil restrictions placed on Catholics during the reign of William III firstly disarmed them and prevented them from keeping a horse worth more than £5; although perhaps understandable in view of the war and the recent circumstances, the right to bear arms and own a good horse were the outward symbols of a gentleman. Secondly, Catholics were forbidden to have their children educated abroad. Many of the Jacobite leaders, like Sarsfield, had been educated at French military academies; so, given the ambiguities of the situation, this too might have been understandable had it not been for the additional prohibition placed on any Roman Catholic keeping a school in Ireland under the penalty of imprisonment and a fine of £20. Thirdly, protestants and Catholics were forbidden to intermarry. Should they defy this prohibition, a protestant woman marrying a Catholic forfeited her possessions and any possible inheritance, while a protestant man who married a Catholic woman was treated as a Catholic unless his wife conformed within a year of the marriage. In cases of doubt certificates of adherence to a protestant Church had to be produced. Any priest or minister marrying such a couple was liable to be fined £20 and spend a year in prison, while, on a successful conviction, an informer received half of the £20 fine.

Severe though these penal statutes were at the death of William, the accession of Anne brought even stricter legislation, for, possibly encouraged by the Queen's sincere support of the Anglican Church, and possibly by the uncertainties inherent in the impending succession question, the penal legislation acquired its most vicious aspects in the 1704 'act to prevent the further growth of popery' which aimed at the annihilation of all Catholic estates and the destruction of Catholic family life. This Act decreed that should the eldest son of a Catholic turn protestant he could secure his traditional inheritance by making his father 'tenant for life'; no Roman Catholic could act as guardian to minors; where the entire family remained Catholic the estate could not be inherited by any one member but must descend in gavelkind and consequently be broken up by being shared among a man's children; no Roman Catholic could purchase a lease in his own or another's name for more than thirty-one years; and finally no Roman Catholic could vote for an M.P. unless he was to take in addition to a simple oath of allegiance, the oath of abjuration, which contained a declaration against transubstantiation and the invocation of the Virgin Mary as well as a declaration that James III 'hath not any right or title to the crown of this realm'. Without any intention or wish to challenge Queen Anne's authority, or the provisions of the Act of Settlement, many protestants as well as Catholics could not agree that James Edward 'hath not any right' – including some Presbyterian ministers who certainly did not wish to have a Catholic sovereign.

Until the passing of this Act, all protestants, whether members of the Church of Ireland or of the other protestant communions, enjoyed the same privileges under the law and the common fruits of the protestant victory. The strongest of the non-conformist protestant groups was the Scottish Presbyterian settlers concentrated in Ulster where they were the dominant religious group. Tough, resilient, independent and frequently convinced of their exclusive rectitude, they represented a threat to the ascendancy which that group was quick to recognise, and throughout the century tenacious to oppose, by maintaining the clause that the English Privy Council added to this bill of 1704, which read: 'provided always, no person shall take benefit of this act as a Protestant, with the intent and meaning thereof, that shall not conform to the Church of Ireland as by law established, and subscribe the declaration and also take and subscribe the oath of abjuration . . .'

There had always been, except in times of extreme danger, a certain degree of friction between the Anglican and Presbyterian communities, and the effect of this clause was to deprive all Presbyterians of any political power and the right to hold any position of trust under the crown, while exposing them to the religious persecution of the Anglican hierarchy. 'And', wrote the Presbyterian historian Reid, 'it was a singular occurrence, an instance, perhaps, of righteous requital, that they themselves after having given their aid in Parliament to carry one of the most cruel of these statutes against the Romanists should, by a clause added to that very statute, be deprived of their own civil rights and subjected in their turn to serious grievances on account of their religion.'

For the decade immediately following the Treaty of Limerick, the presence of a tolerant and Calvinist monarch afforded the Presbyterian community a measure of protection, although evidence for the impending protestant split was already present in the 1690s when Sir Richard Cox, while paying lip-service to toleration for 'all friends to the State', nevertheless considered that 'as there was no test in Ireland, it was necessary for the security of the Established Church to exclude from offices, or any share in the government, all those who would not conform to the Church established by law', and he moved that Presbyterians should be excluded from all public offices, civil or military. This motion was carried by a majority of the Council against the wishes of government. It was only dropped on a petition from the Presbyterians to William III, then campaigning in Flanders. During this decade there were also indications that two other areas of Presbyterian life were liable to attack from the Anglican hierarchy and their supporters in the government: namely, the *regium donum* and the validity of Presbyterian marriages.

Shortly after his accession, William III had confirmed and doubled the *regium donum* or Royal Bounty. This was a sum of money, originally £600, first paid by Charles II in 1672 to encourage the loyalty of the Ulster Presbyterians at the time of the Declaration of Indulgence. The Presbyterian clergy divided the money equally among themselves as an augmentation to their often meagre salaries. Like the Catholic clergy the Presbyterian ministers were poor. During the years 1715 to 1720 there was a succession of bad harvests and in 1720 the General Synod of the Presbyterian Church addressed a letter to its adherents saying, 'it is melancholy to hear that many of our brethren are wanting even the necessaries of life; others are forced to lay down their charge; and others transport themselves to America', and in this year the Rev. McGregor, minister of Aghadowey, emigrated to Massachusetts with a number of his congregation; he was owed £80 but the congregational funds amounted to one shilling!

Emigration to America during the eighteenth century came almost entirely from Ulster. 'No Papists stir', wrote Archbishop King of Dublin in 1718. Ten years later Primate Boulter declared, 'the whole of the North is in a ferment at present, and people engaging one another to go to the *West Indies* . . . the worst is that it affects only protestants and reigns chiefly in the North' and Arthur Young commented during the 1770s that emigrants 'were generally dissenters, very few Churchmen or Catholics'. Most Ulster emigrants did not arrive in America as free men. In addition to religious disabilities, famine, which presupposes poverty, was often the spur to emigration, and a system of indentured servitude was the usual method of financing it. In 1728 Primate Boulter estimated that only one in ten could pay his fare. The cost of a passage to America at the beginning of the century was between £5 and £6. By 1773 advertisements in the *Belfast Newsletter* were quoting £3.5.0 and through increased trade and competition the fare became even lower at the end of the century. Harsh though the indenture system was it offered to many the foundation of a better life. For example, Charles Thomson, the Secretary to the Continental Congress, had emigrated as an indentured servant from Maghera, County Londonderry. Tenacious of purpose and sparing of speech, these emigrants, inured to hardship and adversity, were in a real sense founders of the United States, and many of the virtues of American society were their traditional characteristics.

From about 1700 onwards, Presbyterian clergy were being subjected to prosecutions in the prerogative courts of the established Church on account of the marriages which they were celebrating in accordance with the form and custom of the Church of Scotland. The Anglican Church declared that those so married were living in fornication and that their children were illegitimate. Nevertheless, the marriages were legally valid, though irregularly entered into, and this subjected them to ecclesiastical, but not to civil, penalties. Probate of wills had to be obtained in an ecclesiastical court, and all who refused to accept the established Church's definition of marriage had their children declared illegitimate, and thus subject to disinheritance. This situation continued until 1782, and certain aspects remained until 1844; it was modified by an Act of 1838 which exempted from prosecution those whose marriages had been conducted by clergymen qualified under the 1719 Toleration Act.

The Presbyterians felt the animosity of the Anglican Church most severely during the reign of Queen Anne, for although the government declared that 'the Queen was determined that Dissenters should not be persecuted or molested in the exercise of their religion', nevertheless, at the time of the Queen's death the doors of Presbyterian 'meeting-houses' were nailed up in Antrim, Downpatrick and Rathfriland. Shortly before the Queen's death the Irish Presbyterians had employed a French Protestant minister at the Hanoverian court to assure the Elector of their support, and the accession of George I undoubtedly made life easier for them. Nevertheless, the Hanoverian succession did not bring the Presbyterians all the advantages which they had anticipated. The *regium donum* was restored and increased to £2,000 a year but the sacramental test was not repealed. However, in 1719 a retrospective Act of Indemnity was passed to protect those who had offered military support to the government during the 1715 rebellion in Scotland, when there were fears of a Jacobite invasion of Ireland. Despite the fact that the Irish parliament considered this to be a special indulgence produced by a particular national emergency, the 1719 Indemnity Act was the first of a series, and twenty-four similar Acts were passed during the next fifty years, thus alleviating to some extent, but always on a temporary basis, the restrictions placed upon the Presbyterians during the penal period.

Presbyterian education was officially restricted during

the early part of the century; nevertheless, there were some notable Presbyterian schools, for example that of James McAlpine at Killyleagh. Most Presbyterians, particularly students for the ministry, received their higher education in Scotland, usually at Glasgow University where they came into contact with the leading trends of continental thought. The closeness of this Scottish connection was reflected in the Irish Church's participation in the many theological disputes of the century. By 1725 these had so disrupted the Presbyterian Church in Ireland that Bishop Nicholson told the Archbishop of Canterbury that 'their anti-Trinitarian New Lights have much distracted and disjoined them; so that our churches throughout the whole province fill apace'. In 1756 Wesley wrote that: 'I spoke very plain at Lisburn, both to the vulgar and the small. But between Seceders, old self conceited Presbyterians, New Light men, Moravians, Cameronians and formal Church-men, it is a miracle of miracles if any here bring forth fruit to perfection.'

Although by far the most prominent, the Presbyterians were not the only protestant dissenters in Ireland. Following the revocation of the Edict of Nantes, and the later disbandment of William III's Irish army which contained many Huguenots, there were settlements of French Protestants scattered throughout the country. Around Portarlington lands were granted to the Huguenot General, Henry de Massue, Marquis de Ruvigny and Earl of Galway. Portarlington became the centre of a colony of veterans, who recorded their origin in the French-style houses and a Church service which was conducted in French until 1817. There was a famous school at Portarlington which attracted many of the sons of the Irish nobility and gentry. It included among its pupils a future Lord Lieutenant, the 1st Marquis Wellesley. In Waterford and Cork there were many Huguenot merchants, particularly engaged in the wine trade. Among the prominent Huguenot families were the Crommelins, who were engaged in the linen manufacture in the North, and the great Dublin banking family of the La Touches. In 1692 a Toleration Act was passed in the Huguenots favour, which was continued under Anne and made perpetual during the reign of George I.

The Quakers had a difficult and sometimes bizarre beginning in the seventeenth century, but during the eighteenth they played an important part in the economic, if not the religious, life of the country. They were usually to be found in the more prosperous agricultural and manufacturing communities, as well as in Dublin and the southern ports of Cork and Waterford. They controlled most of the woollen and worsted yarn trade, and they were prominent in the linen industry. In fact their prosperity was such that an American Quaker commented at the end of the century, 'Friends in Ireland seem to live like Princes of the Earth', and certainly few commercial enterprises appear to have operated without their participation.

Another group of dissenters were the Palatines, who were settled in small communities in various parts of the country in accordance with a scheme devised in 1709 to encourage German protestants from the Palatine, rendered homeless by the French wars, to come to Ireland with a view to increasing the protestant population and improving Irish agriculture. The scheme was not entirely successful, but it did leave isolated pockets of German protestants who, like the French, continued their separate traditions for about a century before merging into the population.

Though the separation of the 'Methodists' from the Anglican Church did not take place until the first decade of the nineteenth century, any discussion of religious life in eighteenth-century Ireland would be incomplete without some reference to the numerous missions of John Wesley, who visited Ireland forty-two times between 1747 and 1789. On his final visit to Ireland, Wesley had the satisfaction of feeling that his mission was established. 'Our little Conference began in Dublin . . .', he wrote, 'I had much satisfaction in this Conference; in which, conversing with between forty and fifty Travelling Preachers, I found such a body of men as I hardly believed could have been found together in Ireland; men of so sound experience, so deep piety, and so strong understanding. I am convinced, they are no way inferior to the English Conference, except it be in number.'

No attempt was made to interfere with any of the dissenters except the Presbyterians, who were essentially feared for their numbers, organisation and concentration, as well as for the political implications of their theological views and expansionist ambitions. In 1711 the Queen was informed that the activities of the Presbyterians, 'if not checked, will in time end in the destruction of the constitution both in Church and State'. The Catholic was feared for what he represented; the Presbyterian for what he was. Possibly this partly explains the uncompromising harshness with which the Anglican hierarchy viewed the claims of the Presbyterians throughout the century, while the Presbyterian's resentment, at what he felt to be acts of both injustice and ingratitude, undoubtedly increased his sufferings during the Penal era. Sir Theobald Butler, presenting the case for the Catholics against the 1704 Act, recalling the services of the Dissenters at Londonderry and Enniskillen, remarked that 'if this is all the return they are like to get, it will be but a slender encouragement, if ever occasion should require, for others to pursue their example'.

The sequel to the 1704 Act was that of 1709, 'an act of explaining and amending an act entitled an act to prevent the further growth of popery'. This statute tightened up the previous penal legislation, and added the clause that no Catholic or anyone in trust for them could receive an annuity either for life or a term of years. After 1715 penal legislation which came on to the statute book tended to fill in the system already laid down by the parliaments of William and Anne. For instance, an Act of the English parliament in 1691 had deprived Irish Catholics of the right to sit in the Parliament of Ireland, the Irish Act of 1704 had disfranchised them and finally an Irish Act of 1727 disfranchised protestant electors married to Catholic wives. Perhaps a final comment on this system should be left to Lecky, the great historian of the ascendancy: 'they', he wrote of the Catholic population, 'were educated through long generations of oppression into an inveterate hostility to the law, and were taught to look for redress in illegal violence or secret combination'. Considering the slender economic possessions with which they started the century, 'the operation of these laws alone might have been safely trusted to reduce the Catholic population to complete degradation'.

Irish historians of preceding generations have tended to consider that the existence of a law made its universal application axiomatic. Nevertheless, this view is far from applicable to either England or Ireland in the eighteenth century. Frequently the statute book represented an attempt to substitute moral authority for physical power and the harshness of the law was a reflection of the lack of physical means for controlling public disorder and individual crime in an age which lacked both a police force and adequate prisons. Much of the application of the law lay in the hands of the unpaid J.P.s whose views could be coloured by local interest and sentiment and over whose actions the central government could only exercise a limited control. The extent to which the Penal Code was applied is therefore uncertain and probably varied from time to time; however, there is general agreement among modern historians of the Catholic Church that 'the penal laws were rarely universally applied in their full rigour'. Thus while the iniquity inherent in the existence of the system remains, it must be regarded in its historical context, and the accepted view of its application should be modified in the light of modern research and our increasing knowledge of the methods and restrictions under which eighteenth-century governments operated. For instance, the law against a Catholic owning a horse valued at more than £5 is a restriction which can in practice have affected very few of the Catholic population, especially as the extent of its application is doubtful. Nevertheless, it enjoys an almost unparalleled place in the extensive mythology which surrounds the Penal Code and it is not improbable that its most heinous application has been its use to whip up indignation in subsequent generations of Irish men and women, who have accepted as axiomatic the presence of a law and its application.

The penal legislation against the Catholic Church was aimed particularly at the hierarchy and the regular clergy, both of whom were traditionally more closely linked to the Vatican than the secular clergy. They were, therefore, more open to the accusation of a divided allegiance, a reality in an age saturated in the belief that a man's religious convictions reflected his political views. An Act of 1697 banished 'all Papists exercising any ecclesiastical jurisdiction, and all regulars of the popish clergy out of the kingdom', decreeing that: 'if any of the said ecclesiastical persons shall be at any time after the said 1st of May, 1698, within the kingdom, they and every of them shall suffer imprisonment, until he or they shall be transported beyond the seas; and if any person so transported shall return again into this kindgom, they and every of them shall be guilty of high treason, and suffer and forfeit as in case of high treason.' Anyone coming into the kingdom from abroad after 29 December 1697 was likewise to be imprisoned for a year and then transported; should they return again they would be deemed guilty of high treason for which the punishment was death and forfeiture of goods. Those who harboured such priests would be subject to a fine of £20 for the first offence, £40 for the second, and forfeiture of lands and possessions for the third.

Transportations began early in 1698 and by the end of that year there were in the environs of Paris alone nearly 400 members of religious orders banished from Ireland. They caused considerable consternation to the exiled James II and his Queen, Mary of Modena, who from their slender resources did their best to ameliorate the position of their co-religionists with the generous assistance of the Pope and the Continental Catholic clergy. 'I feel the torture of seeing them with my own eyes dying of want', wrote James II, 'after having shared with them what I needed for my own support'. 'All the regular priests of the Irish mission . . .', said Mary of Modena, 'have already been hunted out of the country. There are just now near four hundred of them in France, and others are in Spain and Portugal, or in Flanders and Italy. I have seen several of them and they have touched me deeply.' Throughout their long exile the Stuarts strained their influence and resources on behalf of the Irish Catholics.

William III was not a little concerned at the international consequences of the Act of 1697, for, as his ally the Emperor Leopold remonstrated: 'It destroys confidence between allies of different religions. Nor will the evil be removed by the plea that the king had to give his sanction, but that he will prevent the laws from being enforced. The king is mortal like other men, and when he is gone these laws may be enforced in their full rigour.' From the time of the Treaty of Limerick, William appears to have given his consent to the insistent demands of the Irish parliament for the enactment of anti-Catholic legislation, but endeavoured to mitigate its application. In adopting this policy he had the support of the Irish Lord Chancellor, Sir Charles Porter, who is perhaps the best example of the moderate opinion which was still represented in the Irish parliament during the 1690s. After a varied career Porter had been appointed Lord Chancellor of Ireland by James II in 1686; Lord Lieutenant Tyrconnell, shortly after his arrival had engineered his dismissal for unspecified reasons. Porter protested to James II, but his protests went unheeded. By December 1688 he had joined the supporters of William, Prince of Orange. After William's victory at the Boyne he was restored to his office of Lord Chancellor in 1690 and on William's departure later that year appointed a Lord Justice. In this capacity he was one of the signatories of the Treaty of Limerick. Porter was noted for his honesty and his genuinely moderate views, which left him open to the opprobrium of both Catholic and Protestant. For instance Lord Lieutenant Capel considered him a Jacobite and assured the English Lord Chancellor Somers that Porter controlled 'the Irish and Jacobite interests' while the country gentry were hostile to him and anxious to censure him in parliament not, the Lord Lieutenant admitted, for either his war record or for signing the articles of Limerick but solely on 'facts committed since his office of Chancellor, generally in favour of Irish papists'. However, Porter managed to defend himself successfully against the Irish House of Commons, although he died shortly afterwards in 1696. During William's reign the position of the secular clergy remained unaffected. However, there had been an order for their enumeration along with that of the regular clergy in 1697, and in consequence the names and addresses of nearly 900 priests were returned.

The death of William and the accession of Queen Anne in 1702 confirmed the Emperor's fears. The bigotry of the English High Church party was now added to the fears and selfishness of their Irish co-religionists, and in 1704 an Act extended the penalties, already imposed on the bishops and regular clergy, to every clergyman of the Catholic religion coming into Ireland after 1 January 1704. The Queen was reluctant to consent to this measure as she felt that it might be 'construed to infringe the articles of Limerick', for by banishing the Catholic bishops and excluding the entry of priests from abroad any legal supply of priests was cut off, and this in time would make it impossible for Catholics to exercise their religion. To meet this objection the bill was limited to a period of fourteen years, but, despite this problem, it was made perpetual in 1709.

This Act was quickly followed by another requiring the registration of all priests then in the country. At the sessions held immediately after 24 June 1704, all secular priests were required to give their name, age, address, parish, the date and place of their ordination and the name of the ordaining prelate. The priest was required to stay in the county in which he was registered, and he had to find two securities of £50 each to guarantee his compliance and good behaviour. Once registered, he was free to carry out his normal duties as a parish priest. So long as the priest was registered, Catholic churches could be, and were, openly resorted to by their congregations. The few bishops who had remained in the country, risking persecution, now registered as parish priests, as did some of the regular clergy, particularly the friars. The theory behind this Act and the 1709 perpetuation of the preceding one was that within a limited number of years the Catholic Church in Ireland, deprived of its clergy, would gradually fade away, – though except for a few extremists like Archbishop King, who held quite simply that 'they or we must be ruined', it is unlikely that the legislators really expected, or wished, for this logical conclusion to their endeavours.

The question of the duality of Catholic loyalty had in fact been a problem since the Reformation. It became an acute one at times when the Pope recognised as the lawful king an individual who was not the actual king. Throughout the penal era there was a direct relation between threatened Jacobite invasion, usually in time of war, and the rigour with which the Penal Code was enforced. For instance, such a crisis occurred in 1708 when the Pretender was expected to invade England. On this occasion a proclamation was issued in Dublin for seizing and jailing all Catholic priests. A few were apprehended, but most went into hiding, and it was during this period that the 1709 bill was framed with a view to tightening the loopholes which had appeared in the existing penal legislation. It offered a reward of £20 for discovering a regular priest, and the large sum of £50 for the discovery of anyone exercising ecclesiastical jurisdiction. Registered priests were now required to take the unacceptable oath of abjuration, and failure to comply with this requirement placed the secular clergy in the same legal position as the regulars. Despite this, there was a mass refusal, for out of the 1,089 clergy registered in 1704 only thirty-three are known to have taken this oath in 1709. Their stand made the Act inoperable, although it meant that the position of all the clergy was now legally vulnerable. However, this was the last Act levied specifically against the clergy, and in practice their position very gradually became established.

From the middle of the eighteenth century the situation of both clergy and laity markedly improved. In 1757 Bishop O'Keefe, the Catholic Bishop of Kildare, declared against the doctrine that the Pope had the right to depose sovereigns, absolve subjects from their oaths, make war on 'heretics' or exercise any temporal power or jurisdiction in Ireland or sanction any immoral act. Two years later the Catholic Association was formed to promote the Catholic cause in a moderate, informed and peaceful manner. By the terms of the Peace of Paris, which, in 1763, concluded the Seven Years War, Great Britain acquired extensive new territories, among them Canada and various West Indian islands. In these new colonies the population was mainly Catholic and their religious liberties were specially secured by the terms of the treaty. Inevitably this situation ameliorated the official attitude and encouraged a greater toleration towards all Britain's Catholic subjects; also, social attitudes had been gradually changing as the views of the French *philosophes* were substituting the deism of the age of reason for the denominational fervour of earlier generations, while in Ireland the generation which had known the terrors of the internecine wars of the seventeenth century had been followed by one which knew only the established ascendancy. Even before the death of James Edward in 1766 a more liberal era was clearly discernible, and from 1768 prayers for the Hanoverian king and the royal family were offered in Catholic churches.

Irish troops fighting for foreign sovereigns had long been a source of annoyance and regret to George II and successive British administrations, but, regardless of personal loyalties, the Penal Laws forbade their recruitment into the British army. However, Catholic marines were recruited during the Seven Years War, and subsequently the religious affiliations of recruits became less strictly regarded, especially by recruiting officers in Leinster, Munster and Connacht. During the first half of the eighteenth century a Catholic middle class had gradually emerged in the towns. As early as 1718 Archbishop King had noticed 'that the Papists . . . have turned themselves to trade, and already engrossed almost all the trade of the kingdom', and having business connections with Europe, they tended to invest their money there. Early in the 1760s an unsuccessful attempt was made to introduce legislation which would allow them to invest in mortgages, and thereby attract their surplus capital back to Ireland. The idea was opposed by the British administration which feared that the notorious prodigality of the Irish gentry would 'give Popish creditors such a control . . . as may in particular times operate very strongly . . .'

The 1770s saw the first legislative relaxation of the Code. An Act of 1772 allowed Catholics to hold leases for 61, instead of 31, years although land so held was supposed to be for purposes of agricultural improvement, for example bog-land. Along with the movement for parliamentary independence went a more liberal outlook: 'the Irish Protestant could never be free', declared Grattan, 'till the Irish Catholic had ceased to be a slave.' In 1774 an Act of parliament allowed Catholics to attest their loyalty in an oath of allegiance accompanied by a declaration similar to Bishop O'Keefe's statement in 1757. Although this Act promised no specific benefits, it was obviously a prelude to concessions. In 1778 Luke Gardiner, afterwards Lord Mountjoy, sponsored a bill which successfully removed the worst aspects of the 1704 Act and allowed Catholics to purchase land-leases for terms of 999 years, abolished the right of the conforming eldest son to dispossess his father and repealed the gavelkind clause, thereby permitting Catholics to consolidate their property.

At the same time an attempt was made to mollify the Presbyterians by repealing the sacramental test which had been added to the 1704 Act in order to prevent Presbyterians from participating in national life in any official capacity. This only succeeded in 1780, as the open support of the Presbyterians for the Americans, then in revolt against Great Britain, was hardly conducive to government favour. Little though they liked the Anglicans, the Presbyterians had retained all the reformation dislike of the Catholic Church, for when further concessions to the Catholics were under consideration in 1782 the Lord Lieutenant, Lord Carlisle, wrote to the Secretary of State, Lord Hillsborough, 'the members who take the lead in this are chiefly independent gentlemen'. Hillsborough, himself an Ulster landowner, and mindful of the anti-Catholic elements in British public opinion as recently expressed in the 1780 Gordon Riots, wrote counselling caution, reminding the viceroy that, 'the prejudices upon matters of this kind in the North of Ireland go to a violence hardly to be credited, and much beyond that of their too near neighbours in Scotland'.

Shortly afterwards, Lord North's government resigned. The new ministry under the Marquis of Rockingham was sympathetic both to the Irish parliament's wish for independence and to the claims of the Irish Catholic. The Duke of Portland was appointed Lord Lieutenant, and during his administration Gardiner introduced a further measure of Catholic relief. To this end, three bills were proposed in 1782, of which two became law. The first of these measures affected both the clergy and the laity. Regarding the laity, the bill tidied up the concessions given in 1778: Catholics who had taken the 1774 oath and declaration could purchase and bequeath lands on the same terms as protestants, provided they were not in parliamentary boroughs, and a number of vexatious laws, such as the famous one, which compelled a Catholic to accept a protestant's offer of £5 for his horse, were repealed. The ecclesiastical clauses of the bill rescinded the laws making it penal for members of the Catholic hierarchy or the regular orders to live in the country and requiring priests to register. At the same time, the bill reaffirmed the laws against proselytism, conversion to Catholicism, forbidding Catholic priests from assuming ecclesiastical ranks and titles or officiating outside their parishes, and all unestablished churches from having steeples and bells. The second bill was mainly concerned with the guardianship and education of Catholic children. Catholics could now become schoolmasters or tutors provided that they took the 1774 oath, subscribed to the declaration, received a licence from the Anglican bishop of the diocese, and instructed only Catholic children. A Catholic university, college or endowed school was still forbidden, but Catholic laymen could act as guardians to Catholic children. A third bill to legalise marriages between Catholics and protestants was defeated. At the same time another bill gave Presbyterian and other dissenting ministers the right to celebrate valid marriages among their adherents, a right which English dissenters did not receive until 1836.

In the decade following the American war, the conservative liberalism which had produced Gardiner's reforms, declined before the aggressive radicalism of those influenced by the French Revolution. The Catholic movement, although basically independent of either, was inevitably affected by both. The dichotomy between the liberal and radical elements of the reform movement was reflected in the 1791 split in the Catholic Committee between the old aristocratic-conservative approach and the new radical-democratic methods. The former were anxious to protest their loyalty and trust to the ultimate justice of their cause; the latter were anxious to join with the dissenters in more aggressive forms of political activity. The French Revolution had virtually closed the possibility of a career in Catholic Europe as an outlet for Irish ambition abroad, while increasing prosperity at home emphasised the restrictions still binding the Irish Catholics. For example, they were still excluded from higher education as were English Catholics, and, with the exception of medicine, from a professional career. They remained similarly excluded from local and national politics.

At the beginning of 1792, the reorganised Catholic Committee petitioned the king. Rather than following the customary procedure of transmitting their petition through the Lord Lieutenant, they sent it directly to England with a delegation led by the Dublin merchant, John Keogh. In London they were well received, but their deviation from the traditional channel of communications reflected the Catholic Committee's increasing alienation from the Irish administration. The position of the viceroy was difficult, for his principal duty was to obtain the acquiescence of the Irish parliament to the policy of the British administration, and the majority of the Irish parliament were becoming increasingly recalcitrant over the question of further concessions to the Catholics. These, in the interests of imperial justice and national unity, the British government was not only willing but even anxious to grant, as they had recently rescinded most of the laws restricting the liberties of English Catholics. To this end the Secretary of State, Henry Dundas, wrote to Lord Lieutenant Westmorland: 'it is essentially necessary as well on grounds of justice as sound policy, to give a favourable ear to the fair claims of the Catholics of Ireland . . . The Roman Catholics form the great body of the inhabitants of the kingdom of Ireland, and as such are entitled to the communication of all such advantages as can be given to them without danger to the existing establishment and to the general interests of the Empire.'

The terrors of the French Revolution and the concessions already granted frightened the more conservative elements in the Irish parliament, who were always aware of their numerical weakness, as Chief Secretary Hobart pointed out to Dundas: 'if you are to maintain a Protestant ascendancy,' he wrote, 'it must be by substituting influence for numbers. The weight of England in the Protestant scale will at all times turn the balance, but if ever the Catholics are persuaded that the Protestants are not certain of English support, they will instantly think it worth their while to hazard a conflict.'

Against this background the Catholic Committee became increasingly more radical and more insistent in its demands. From 1790 to 1792 they had employed Richard Burke as their adviser, possibly hoping for the wisdom and experience of the brilliant and influential father rather than the more moderate abilities of the son, who in addition lacked both tact and discretion. In 1792, after many vicissitudes, they broke with Richard Burke and his liberal conservative connotations and later in the year appointed as their salaried secretary a young Protestant lawyer, Theobald Wolfe Tone, who in 1791 had very ably attacked the remaining Penal Laws in 'An argument on behalf of the Catholics of Ireland'. Tone's ambition was to unite Irishmen of every creed in a movement for radical reform, and to this end he had in 1791 helped to found the United Irishmen. Among the influential members of the Catholic Association who had reservations about Tone's political ambitions was John Keogh, who refused to join the United Irishmen.

Under strong pressure from Westminster, the Irish parliament reluctantly and grudgingly gave way and consented to the 1792 Catholic Relief Bill. This Act allowed Catholics to practise at the Bar and hold legal positions below the rank of King's Counsel and exclusive of the Bench. Catholics could now marry protestants and educate their children as they pleased; a licence was no longer required to hold a school and restrictions on the number of apprentices belonging to Catholic tradesmen were also removed. Entrance to the university, the right to endow colleges, universities or schools and the long-sought political rights came with a further Relief Bill in 1793. This Act restored the parliamentary franchise to the Catholics on the same terms as the protestants and allowed them a similar equality of service on grand or petty juries. They could now become magistrates and members of corporations. Finally any legal restriction or disability regarding personal property was removed and, subject to the customary property qualification, Catholics could now carry arms. Not surprisingly, the Catholic population did not feel mollified by the ungracious manner in which the concessions had been given, so they failed to achieve the purpose which the British government had intended, and agitation for complete emancipation now began.

At this juncture, the Duke of Portland, who had encouraged the 1782 concessions, joined Pitt in a coalition government, bringing with him the conservative section of the old Whig Party, which had finally split over the French Revolution. As part of this arrangement Earl Fitzwilliam was sent to Ireland, and in this delicate situation his lack of administrative experience and failure to comprehend the nature and powers of his office was disastrous. Imbued with Grattan's views, he sincerely wished to unite the people of Ireland into a nation and he felt that the way to do this was to grant Catholic Emancipation immediately. He made no secret of his unauthorised intentions, and at the same time he dismissed the heads of the 'civil service'.

Horrified at his activities, the British government recalled him within six weeks of his arrival. Although Fitzwilliam's intentions had been excellent, irreparable damage had been done by raising Catholic hopes before the Protestant ascendancy could be persuaded to consent to their wishes. Catholic resentment deepened, and was not allayed by such gestures as the foundation and endowment of Maynooth College in 1795. The ultra-Protestant elements in the ascendancy were further alarmed and endeavoured to safeguard their position by every possible means, including persuading the uneven mind of King George III that such a concession would be contrary to his coronation oath to protect the Anglican Church. Catholic resentment flared into rebellion in 1798, and two years later the Protestant ascendancy sought the security of the Act of Union. Pitt's conciliatory plan for union with emancipation was destroyed. The Irish problem had once again come full circle.

Despite its pre-eminent position the situation of the Established Church in the eighteenth century was difficult. Its spiritual rôle was largely impossible while its exposure to the demands and temptations of the state was immense. 'The bulk of the common people in Ireland', wrote Archbishop King in 1715, 'are either Papists or Dissenters, equally enemies to the Established Church: but the gentry are in general conformable, and the Church interest apparently lies in them.' Property not population was the key-stone of political power in the eighteenth century, and even had there been no penal legislation lack of property would have ensured the political subservience of all non-conformists, Catholic or protestant, to the land-owning section of the community which by 1688 was already predominantly Anglican. Their numerical slenderness created many difficulties, especially as they were inevitably spread throughout the country and not, like the Ulster Presbyterians, mainly concentrated in one area. This spread of population combined with the Anglican Church's position as the established Church posed grave religious, economic and administrative problems.

As the established Church, the Church of Ireland had a duty to make provision for the religious welfare of the entire population. Even had they all been resident the number of clergy was, throughout the century, totally inadequate for the task to which the Church aspired. There were probably between 600 and 800 clergy at the beginning of the century and about 1,100 in 1800, meanwhile the population had increased from about $2\frac{1}{2}$ millions to approximately $5\frac{1}{2}$ millions. The financial resources of the Church were similarly over-stretched, for although it was sustained by the tithes of the entire nation, in many parishes the tithes were impropriated or held by laymen. In 1760 Sir James Caldwell calculated that there 'were not more than 550 officiating clergy in the whole kingdom, and the greater part of these are poor, miserable curates whose whole income is at most but £40 a year'. The wealth of the Church was very unevenly divided, and even within the divisions of the higher and lower clergy there were wide discrepancies, for instance episcopal incomes varied between £2,000 and £7,000 a year as the emoluments of a bishopric were made up from the tithes and lands attached to each see.

Writing in the middle of the century, Theophilus Bolton,

Archbishop of Cashel from 1730 to 1744 and previously Bishop of Clonfert and of Elphin, considered that 'a true Irish bishop had nothing more to do than to eat, drink, grow fat, rich and die'. Similar discrepancies in the performance of their calling existed among the lower clergy. Carleton in *Valentine M'Clutchy* ironically contrasts the vicar who spends his time worshipping the king in London while his poor curate worships God in the country. Ireland's proximity to England made Irish patronage, ecclesiastical as well as civil, particularly attractive to recipients whose talents, connections or situation made it unlikely that they would be adequately rewarded in England. This placed a heavy burden on the resources of the Irish Church, both materially and psychologically. Following the death of Archbishop Boyle in 1703, every Primate of All Ireland during the century was an Englishman, and two, Archbishop Boulter, 1724–42, and Archbishop Stone, 1747–64, were ecclesiastical servants of the Crown whose careers recall those of Laud and Wolsey in an earlier age. In the first half of the century the bishops, as lords spiritual, were the most stable and often the decisive element in the House of Lords; the temporal peers had not numerically recovered from the revolution, or been swollen to the inflated proportions which they acquired by the end of the century. In order to ensure the bishops' loyalty to the government Archbishop Boulter preferred that there should be at least an equal if not a predominant representation of Englishmen on the bench of bishops. In 1727 he informed the Lord Lieutenant 'that if some person be not now brought over from *England* to the bench, there will be thirteen *Irish* to nine *English* Bishops here, which we think will be a dangerous situation'. These ecclesiastics tended in turn to exercise their rights of patronage in favour of their English friends and relatives.

Notoriety attracts more attention than virtue, and there were many Anglican clergy and prelates who resisted the pressures of the age and the temptations of their position. Archbishop King, for example, was a devout Anglican and a conscientious bishop and archbishop. He reorganised the diocese of Derry following the Jacobite wars: 'I restored as much as I could ecclesiastical discipline,' he wrote in his autobiography, 'I exhorted the clergy much to frugality sobriety and diligence.' On another occasion he declared that 'that humour of clergymen living near Dublin, declining remote and barbarous countries, as they call them, is by no means to be indulged; for 'tis plain that this is to prefer the clergyman's ease to the salvation of the people'. Another learned and devout bishop was the philosopher, George Berkeley, Bishop of Cloyne from 1734 to 1753, who endeavoured to cure his flock from a variety of ills with tar water, while at the same time he tried to improve their circumstances by establishing a spinning school for the instruction of the children and a workhouse for the destitute.

Towards the end of the century Samuel Burdy in his *Life of the Rev. Philip Skelton, 1707–87* gives a picture of a learned and virtuous country clergyman: 'Mr Skelton', he writes, 'entered on the cure of Monaghan with that eager zeal for the salvation of souls, which a warm sense of duty only could inspire . . . He laboured hard in his ministry: he visited them from house to house, without distinction of sect; he conversed with them freely, mingling entertainment with his instruction . . . His life was conformable to his preaching . . . His fixed salary for the cure was £40' and there is a considerable amount of evidence to indicate that a salary of £40 to £50 was fairly usual for clergymen in this type of parish. Considering that many of these men had families to support they can have been very little if any better off than their Catholic or Presbyterian counterparts.

The secular position and the Erastian tendencies of the eighteenth-century Church of Ireland were largely inescapable. As early as 1715 Archbishop King was aware that the position of the Church, which he had fought so hard to secure, was not entirely beneficial to it, as he remarked to a friend: 'I never observed the countenance of a government to add much to the security of the Church. I will maintain that under King William, when we did not reckon ourselves great favourites, we had advanced our congregations more every four years than we did under the four years of the late management here (1710–14), in which I fear we lost ground: the diligence, piety, humility, and prudent management of the clergy, when they had nothing else to trust to, proving much stronger motives to gain the people than the favour of the government, which put the clergy on other methods and made them odious to the people.' Five years later he was writing to the Archbishop of Tuam 'as to the Government, I think it advisable that the clergy in their sermons should avoid meddling with matters of State, and keep themselves to the articles of our holy religion and the duties of Christianity: for the clergy, by mixing in matters of politicks, have more than once, in my time, brought themselves into many inconveniences, without any advantage to the Church'. Nevertheless, the political position of the Church of Ireland, numerically weak and dependent on the government, made it impossible for it to develop along the lines that King wished. This was to be its enduring tragedy, just as the persecution and sufferings of the Catholics and to a lesser extent of the Presbyterians were to permanently sustain and strengthen their people.

3 The Age of Molyneux and Swift, c. 1692–1730

BEFORE considering the principal developments of political life in eighteenth-century Ireland it is perhaps useful to outline the political and administrative framework within which they took place. This will give some indication of the restrictions operating on both the British administration and the Irish parliament, thereby making certain developments more comprehensible. The political context within which the Protestant ascendancy operated was a narrow one and their dependence upon and proximity to England combined with their numerical slenderness – they were probably not more than a tenth of the population – to emphasise, sometimes to grotesque proportions, many of the features which were an integral part of eighteenth-century political administration in both countries. Possibly the features which have been the greatest cause of comment were the prevalence of 'rotten' boroughs, which represented the property of the proprietor rather than the views of the inhabitants, the extensive use of government patronage for the benefit of M.P.s and their relatives, and the lavish creation of peerages, particularly during the reign of George III, when, for instance, between 1767 and 1785 alone, fifty new peerages were created.

The dependent nature of Irish government was demonstrated by its inbuilt problem : the separation of the executive from the legislature. This divorce between the source of policy and the financial resources necessary for its implementation, gave a particular value to the means available for creating some form of political cohesion between these two elements whose accord was essential to the government of Ireland. The Irish parliament had no control whatsoever in the appointment of the Lord Lieutenant, nevertheless the successful operation of government depended upon his ability to persuade it to pass the legislation necessary to implement his policy. At the same time the number of seats which the administration permanently controlled in the House of Commons was very small, being confined to the eight members returned for the four constituencies controlled by the archbishop of Armagh and the bishops of Ferns, Ossory and Clogher – and the bishop's influence could be challenged at Clogher. Two indirect means remained: a judicious distribution of patronage in the shape of pensions, places and peerages, and arousing the ascendancy's fear of offending England upon whose support, against the hostility of the majority of the population, it depended in times of crisis. The attitude of the Irish parliament towards the Lord Lieutenant was frequently that which Archbishop King expressed to Dean Swift in 1711 when he remarked that, 'I reckon every chief governor who is sent here comes with a design to serve first those who sent him; and that our good only must be so far considered as it is subservient to the main design'.

Ireland was the largest of England's medieval possessions to survive into the modern era as a dependency, and she shared the forms if not the substance of England's constitutional development. The government of Ireland was by 'king, lords and commons in parliament assembled'; the names were the same, but because the kingdom of Ireland was a dependent kingdom the rôles were different. Nevertheless, Ireland was the only subordinate British possession to possess a parliament, complete with a House of Lords, instead of a Representative Assembly. From 1495 until its amendment in 1782, the most celebrated of Irish statutes, Poynings' Law, restricted the legislative function of the Irish parliament to consenting to, or rejecting, bills which had previously been approved by the English Privy Council, thereby preventing any possibility of a legislative conflict between two countries ultimately administered by the same king. This Act had been modified during the reign of Mary I to allow the Irish Privy Council to transmit legislation formulated after parliament had met. During the seventeenth century the Irish parliament had gradually established the custom of introducing legislation in a form known as 'Heads of Bills'. These differed from normal bills only in the opening words, which were, 'we pray that it may be enacted', and not 'be it enacted'. The 'Heads of Bills' then went to the Irish Privy Council where they could be altered or suppressed. Thus, as the Lord Chancellor of Great Britain, Lord Camden, pointed out in 1767, 'the council in that country is an assembly of equal importance with either of the branches of the Legislature'.

Legislation officially commenced in the Privy Council and if, when the 'Heads of Bills' were sent to them, the Council did not suppress them they became bills; the original formula being replaced with the traditional 'be it enacted', and, sealed with the great seal of Ireland, they were transmitted to the English Privy Council which had similar powers of alteration or rejection. Such bills, as were subsequently returned to Ireland, carried the great seal of Great Britain – prior to 1707 the great seal of England. They were then reintroduced into the Irish parliament, where they could be either accepted or rejected, but not in any way amended. If they were accepted by both Houses the Lord Lieutenant gave the royal assent, and they became law. In 1782 Poynings' Law was amended in such a way that subsequent legislation was introduced directly into either House of Parliament. Nevertheless, even after 1782, Irish bills remained subject to review by the British Privy Council and to the royal veto in common with the legislative Acts of all Great Britain's overseas possessions. As in

England membership of the Privy Council had both honorary and executive implications, and the operation of Poynings' Law undoubtedly gave additional prestige, and therefore additional desirability, to membership of the Irish Privy Council.

Between 1703 and 1767 the Lord Lieutenant was absent for long periods during his viceroyalty. When he left the country three Lords Justices were appointed each with a salary of £200 per month to carry on the routine administration and to secure the necessary majority to implement any policy which he brought over when he returned to open parliament. For this purpose they were allowed a wide exercise of royal patronage and control over the Castle secretariat. The commission of Lords Justices was most frequently made out in favour of the Primate, the Speaker of the House of Commons and the Chancellor, who usually presided over the House of Lords. Occasionally one of these officials might be replaced by a prominent nobleman, like Lord Kildare in 1756, and during the reign of George I the Whig Archbishop of Dublin, William King, was systematically appointed instead of the Tory Primate, Archbishop Lindsay of Armagh. The advantage of this system was that these politicians were either Irishmen and great borough proprietors, like Speakers Conolly and Boyle, or Englishmen who had decided to spend their lives and make their careers in Ireland, like the Primates throughout the century and the Chancellors between 1725 and 1790. They, therefore, created to some extent a natural bridge between the executive and the legislature. The disadvantage was that they came to control the machinery of government almost completely, and the line between their personal and their official patronage became so blurred that they reduced the viceroy to a cypher who 'may parade but must submit'.

Largely created in the seventeenth century the eighteenth-century House of Commons was composed of 300

VOTERS

- Under 1000
- 1000 – 1999
- 2000 – 2999
- 3000 – 3999
- Over 4000

Meath	Longford	Kildare	Kilkenny
1 Kells	Granard	Naas	Gowran
2 Athboy	St Johnston	Kildare	Kilkenny
3 Trim	Longford	Harristown	Irishtown
4 Navan	Lanesborough	Athy	Callan
5 Ratoath			Thomastown
6 Duleek			Knocktopher
7			Inistioge

A Map showing the size of the county electorates before 1793 where known and the constituencies returning M.P.s to the Irish parliament.

members returned for 150 double-member constituencies, representing 32 counties, 117 parliamentary boroughs and Dublin university. In most boroughs the return of members to parliament was vested in the corporation. These from the reign of Anne were exclusively Anglican, and because of the slender Anglican electorate frequently composed of absentees, a situation condoned by the 'Newtown Act' of 1747. Consequently there was no structural difference between the corporation of the 'great and opulent' town of Belfast and Bannow 'which retains *only the name*, being *totally uninhabited*'. Membership of the vast majority of these corporations was vested in either the friends or the dependent tenants of a single individual and as the Commissioners for Municipal Corporations reported in 1835: 'the influence thus acquired became regarded as the property of its possessor and was transmitted as part of the family inheritance to his descendants'. This influence could also be bought and sold, for instance the borough of Carrick with 13 non-resident burgesses was 'Mr Robert Clements Borough – his father purchased it off the late General St George for £5,000', possibly about 1763. Increasing political interest ensured that both boroughs and borough representation became very much more expensive during the last three decades of the century. During the 1770s and 1780s a seat for a single octennial parliament cost on average about £2,500 to £3,000. The idea that parliamentary representation was a species of property was so widely accepted that in 1800 £1,260,000 was paid in compensation to the patrons of the eighty boroughs which were totally disfranchised by the Act of Union. All the borough-owners who could prove their 'ownership' received £15,000 per constituency or £7,500 per seat. Even the established Church was compensated for the loss of St Canice *alias* Irishtown which had been controlled by the Bishop of Ossory, and the then bishop made a personal claim for this compensation on the grounds that his predecessor had for more than a century, by following the directions of the government in returning members to parliament, been rewarded by translation to more desirable sees!

The nature of the representative system presented certain problems to the administration for its control was both concentrated and diffuse. Therefore, for the administration to exert influence over it required an application of patronage which was similarly concentrated and extensive. For instance in 1783, 11 peers returned 51 M.P.s and 3 commoners a further 11 M.P.s, while 25 peers and 33 commoners each returned 2 M.P.s and 6 peers and 26 or possibly 31 commoners each returned 1 M.P. By this calculation 109 individuals were involved in returning 215 M.P.s. The executive could only permanently influence the return of the 8 M.P.s for the bishops' boroughs. Nevertheless, the administration did acquire a certain amount of transient electoral influence, as occasionally borough-owners who wished to improve their position with the government, the source of all honours and patronage, would ask the Lord Lieutenant to nominate a purchaser whom they might even bring in at a reduced rate, as in 1776 when Charles O'Hara was returned by Thomas Knox, later Lord Welles, for his borough of Dungannon 'by Lord Harcourt's means paying only £1,000'; while 'whenever a judgeship or peerage was asked for any person in parliament,' stated the Chief Secretary in 1762, 'an offer was constantly made to government for the seat which should be vacated'. Twenty years later, just before the 1783 election, Lord Lieutenant Northington was writing that, 'it is our intention first to recommend the old four (for peerages), Clement, Tonson, Matthew and Pomeroy, we have two seats from the second, I hope two from the first, one from Matthew and the Duke of Leinster, strong as he is, is to be had by the other'. Apart from seats acquired by these methods the administration had to build its majority by a judicious distribution of patronage among the greater and lesser borough proprietors for 'a sufficient following must', as Lord Townshend declared, 'in this as in all countries be held by government to carry on business'. This was the context within which Irish parliamentary government operated throughout the eighteenth century and the constitutional amendments of 1782 emphasised rather than altered the situation.

An Act of the English parliament passed in 1691 required that the members of both Houses of the Irish parliament should subscribe to a declaration against certain specifically Catholic doctrines, consequently the parliament which met on 5 October 1692 was entirely Protestant as well as overwhelmingly Anglican. The first parliament called by William and Mary displayed a mixture of theories and emotions which were partly the result of the contemporary situation, partly a reflection of the political philosophy which surrounded the 1688 Revolution in England, and partly an expression of the inherent beliefs of all educated in the English political tradition although resident overseas. Their ideas were expounded by William Molyneux, M.P. for Dublin University in both the parliaments of William III, in *The case of Ireland's being bound by Acts of Parliament in England stated* published in 1699, and Jonathan Swift's *Drapier's Letters,* particularly the fourth letter, published in 1724.

Neither Molyneux nor Swift considered the Catholic population as relevant to their arguments: 'as to the people of this Kingdom,' wrote Swift, 'they consist either of *Irish Papists*; who are as inconsiderable in Point of Power, as the Women and children; or of *English Protestants,* who love their brethren of that Kingdom; although they may possibly sometimes complain, when they think they are hardly used'; Molyneux's argument is more indirect and more specious: 'now 'tis manifest', he declares, 'that the great body of the present People of *Ireland* are the Proginy of the *English* and *Britains* . . . and there remains but a meer handful of the Ancient *Irish* at this day; . . . so that if I, or any Body else claim the like Freedoms with the natural born *subjects* of *England,* as being descended from them, it will be impossible to prove the contrary,' and his argument continues, 'if . . . it be concluded that the Parliament of *England* may bind *Ireland*; it must also be allowed that the People of *Ireland* ought to have their *Representatives* in the Parliament of *England.* And this I believe we should be willing enough to embrace; but this is a happiness we can hardly hope for.' In this last extract Molyneux shows his feeling that a way existed for an attack on the firmly held belief in the sanctity of property through taxation without representation, for, he declared, 'to tax me without Consent, is little better, if at all, than down-right Robbing me'. This idea was in fact far from new when the American colonists made it a slogan in the years before the American Revolution.

During the late 1690s and early 1700s, approximately in the period between the embargo on the export of Irish woollens and the Scottish Act of Union, there was a strong inclination in Ireland for a similar Anglo-Irish union, but because the Irish Act of 33 Henry VIII made the crown of Ireland dependent upon 'the imperial crown of England', Ireland was automatically bound by the English Act of Settlement and therefore could not exercise the same bargaining power as that possessed by Scotland over the succession question. Much of Molyneux's political writing reflects his friendship with John Locke, whose *Essay on the True original extent and end of civil government* exerted an immense influence over his contemporaries and made a major contribution to the philosophical background of the English Revolution of 1688.

In addition to these concepts of its inherent rights and liberties the parliament which Lord Lieutenant Sydney met in 1692 was a body in which fear and terror had reacted in anger and a desire for revenge. Under these circumstances not only was it impossible for the viceroy to persuade parliament to confirm the treaty of Limerick, but the anxiety of the Irish politicians to establish their constitutional position as they envisaged it led to demands which included a Habeas Corpus Act, the rejection of a government-sponsored Mutiny Bill, because it was perpetual and not under the annual review of parliament as in England, and finally to the rejection of a bill of supply 'because it did not take its rise in the House of Commons'. This last rejection contained an indirect attack on Poynings' Law and Lord Sydney was instructed to prorogue parliament, having first recorded his formal rebuke. Parliament had sat for less than a month when Lord Sydney carried out his instructions and prorogued it on 3 November 1692; subsequent prorogations prevented its meeting again before its dissolution on 26 June 1693.

During its brief session the first Irish parliament of the post-Revolution era had not only engrossed itself in constitutional issues to the detriment of other business, but had criticised the distribution of forfeited estates, and indicated that any policy other than one of rigid severity towards the defeated Roman Catholics would arouse overwhelming opposition from the Anglican gentry. The country gentlemen dominated the House of Commons and against their fears and prejudices the moderating influence of the Lord Chancellor, Sir Charles Porter, was powerless. The Lord Chancellor's supporters comprised the professional group in the House. A few years later Lord Lieutenant Capel, who was suspicious of Porter's moderation, declared that his party was composed of the 'lawyers, attorneys and solicitors, that make a considerable part of the House. The Commissioners of the Revenue and collectors are all on his side; many gentlemen likewise that have suits depending in his court; and all the Irish and Jacobite interests are entirely at his devotion.' Throughout the eighteenth century the majority of the House of Commons was composed of the country gentry and their views inevitably dominated it. Nevertheless, the House always had a number of lawyers as their professional consequence at all levels was greatly assisted by having a seat in parliament, and for men like Anthony Malone, John Hely-Hutchinson and Henry Grattan a legal education was largely a preliminary to a political career.

Until 1697, when peace was made at Ryswick, England and the Netherlands were at war with France, the refuge of James II and the majority of the Jacobite aristocrats who supported him. William III and his English ministers were, therefore, anxious to placate the Irish parliament during this period of national emergency. When a new parliament was elected in 1695, a new Lord Lieutenant, Lord Capel, was sent over to implement a conciliatory policy reflected in certain popular appointments, such as that of Alan Broderick to the office of Solicitor-General, and in the beginning of new penal legislation against the Catholics which marked the failure of William's hopes for toleration. The Irish parliament responded to these overtures by placing its constitutional claims in abeyance, voting supplies, and in 1697 it finally agreed to confirm a mutilated version of the Treaty of Limerick. Unlike the parliaments of the eighteenth century which before 1783 met biennially, this parliament met annually until its prorogation in 1698 prior to its dissolution on 14 June 1699.

After the cessation of hostilities, the primitive agrarian Irish economy had recovered rapidly. By 1697 the ever-jealous English merchants considered that the export of Irish woollen goods overseas might constitute a threat to this important area of their trade. They demanded that the mercantilist system should be extended to forbid its competition and this was done by an Act of the English parliament in 1698. This Act had two indirect consequences: the encouragement of the Irish linen manufacture by the administration and the parliaments of both countries, and the statement of Ireland's constitutional claims contained in Molyneux's pamphlet, which aroused the immediate and emphatic condemnation of the English House of Commons.

The reign of Queen Anne was dominated by foreign war and the succession question; issues which were partially provoked and greatly aggravated by Louis XIV's acknowledgement and support of Prince James Edward's claims to be James III, while Queen Anne's known devotion to, and support of, the Anglican Church encouraged the emerging ascendancy to consolidate their position particularly in the repressive and exclusive penal legislation of 1704 and 1709. As the reign progressed the importance of the succession question intensified. The element of uncertainty which this issue increasingly generated found expression in the acrimony which characterised political behaviour in both the British and the Irish parliaments.

In both countries these political debates had religious overtones. In Ireland they centred round such issues as the repeal of the sacramental test attached to the 1704 Act which disqualified Presbyterian dissenters from holding office; for instance in April 1708 Swift, who was then in England, commented to one of his correspondents that, 'here has the *Irish* Speaker been soliciting to get the *Test Clause* repealed by an Act here', while during the following November Archbishop King assured Swift, who shared his High Church views, that 'the reason of their applying in *Great Britain* is because they see little reason to hope for success here; and if I can judge the sense of gentlemen that compose the Parliament, they never seem to be farther from the humour of gratifying them'. The Speaker was Alan Broderick who espoused the Whig-Dissenting line in Ireland as did his eventual successor William Conolly, who had made a great fortune over the recent sales of confiscated lands, while the Tory–High Church view was represented by men like Sir Richard Levinge. Nevertheless, Sir Richard Cox spoke for all Irish Tories when he declared that he was 'perfectly Hanoverian as to the succession', and Cox's support of Sir Constantine Phipps, the Tory Lord Chancellor with Jacobite inclinations, was probably encouraged by his enmity to the Brodericks. Many Churchmen like Archbishop King were Tory in their ecclesiastical outlook, but Whig in their political views. The Whig and Tory factions in the British administrations of the reign were revealed by the appointment of the Whig Earl of Wharton as viceroy in 1708, and in the recurring appointment of the Tory 2nd Duke of Ormonde, 1703–5, 1710–11 and 1713. The dominant position of the Tories after 1710 was indicated by the appointment of Sir Constantine Phipps as Lord Chancellor of Ireland and in his commission as a Lord Justice during the absence of Ormonde in 1711 and 1712.

Concerned at the strength of the Irish opposition and anxious to consolidate their power, in May 1713 the Tory ministers in England decided to advise the Queen to dissolve the Irish parliament. A new one was immediately summoned to meet on 25 November under the viceroyalty of the Duke of Shrewsbury. The arrangement of the general election was entrusted to Lord Chancellor Phipps, who prepared the ground carefully and based his campaign on the slogan 'Queen and Church'. The Whigs countered by accusing the administration of dividing the Protestants, supporting pro-Catholic policies and even encouraging Jacobites. Some colour was given to these accusations by the election of nine recent converts: Garrett Bourke, George Browne, Cornelius Callaghan, Darby Egan, Redmond Everard, Patrick French, Denis Daly, George Mathew and Charles Plunkett.

However, following the election the Tories calculated that they had secured 180 out of the 300 parliamentary seats and that the balance of the House was now in their favour. Confident of this majority, when parliament met the government nominated Sir Richard Levinge for election as Speaker. The opposition, led by William Conolly nominated Alan Broderick. Broderick won by four votes and his victory was followed by an almost equally disastrous defeat for the government when Anderson Saunders, their candidate for Chairman of the Committee of Elections was defeated by six votes. Confronted by these unexpected defeats the Tories complained that their supporters had been lax in attendance and that some of them, including the Chief Secretary, had even voted for John Forster the suave Whig candidate for the chairmanship of the Committee of Elections. Worse was to follow as the opposition moved on to the attack. The Dublin election had ended in a riot, the army had been called out and a man had been killed. This event was fully discussed by the House of Commons and the debate concluded by a series of resolutions one of which stated that Phipps' servant was 'a chief fomentor of and instrument in' creating the riot. They then turned to attack the Chancellor himself and Phipps only escaped their censure by the intervention of the House of Lords.

A month after the 1713 parliament met the uninvolved, middle-of-the-way viceroy, the Duke of Shrewsbury, adjourned parliament declaring that, 'my temper is so unfit to join with either of these parties that I hope Her Majesty will recall me and name some other Governor more fitly qualified for this tempestuous station'. He then sent for the opposition leaders and warned them that they were not to meddle with the succession question, which belonged to the parliament of Great Britain, to which admonition Speaker Broderick replied that the Irish parliament had as absolute a right to legislate for Ireland as the British parliament had to legislate for Britain, and that the Irish Commons were determined to secure the Protestant succession. Broderick's constitutional view was contrary to the 1542 Act of the Irish parliament which had declared that 'this land of Ireland is depending and belonging . . . to the imperial crown of England'. Shrewsbury then prorogued parliament until 14 August 1714 and returned to England. Before the prorogation ended parliament was dissolved by the death of the Queen on 1 August. The last act of the dying Queen had been to appoint Lord Lieutenant Shrewsbury as Lord Treasurer of Great Britain and it was Shrewsbury who, acknowledging the Protestant succession and adhering to the Act of Settlement, proclaimed George I King of Great Britain and Ireland.

During Shrewsbury's viceroyalty the Primacy had become vacant following the death of Archbishop Marsh in 1713. Anxious to rebuff the Whigs and indicate their confidence in Lord Chancellor Phipps, the British administration had insisted on appointing Thomas Lindsay, Bishop of Raphoe, to the archbishopric of Armagh instead of the Whig Archbishop King of Dublin. However, the Hanoverian succession secured the *de facto* dominance of King as the leading ecclesiastical figure in Ireland, and it was King who commented that the fundamental difference between English and Irish politics during the reign of Queen Anne was that the English were concerned with whom, and what kind of person, would advise the sovereign in the government of the country, while the Irish were dominated by the need to secure their estates 'which are claimed by the forfeitors and nothing can restore them but the Pretender . . . Here', declared King, 'is the true source of the zeal and violence of the Protestants of Ireland.'

Thus the immediate completeness of their victory in 1692, combined with the long-drawn-out uncertainty as to its permanence, gave the insecure and frightened Anglican parliament little occasion, or inclination, to learn that a judicious magnanimity is perhaps an essential ingredient for the consolidation of victory in a country in which the victors represent so small a proportion of the community. At the same time, the flight of the Catholic aristocracy and their association with Jacobite powers abroad left the mass of the people an easy prey to the fear and greed of the victors, whose worst fears were confirmed by the Roman Curia's acknowledgement of James III and its subsequent acceptance of his advice on Irish ecclesiastical affairs until his death in 1766.

Ireland, unlike Scotland, did not rebel either in 1715 or 1745 and the peace which followed the Hanoverian succession ushered in a period of relative security and tranquillity. As the land settlement became increasingly permanent, the original harshness of the Penal Code became blunted, nevertheless the laws remained and were in some cases developed to their logical conclusion, for instance in the 1727 Act which removed the last vestiges of Catholic influence over the parliamentary franchise. Similarly the long years of peace brought no relaxation in the Anglican parliament's hostility towards protestant dissent.

The years following 1715 saw consecutively bad harvests and although in 1719 a Toleration Act followed by a series of Indemnity Acts allowed protestant non-conformists an uncertain respite from the 1704 Act, repeated attempts to repeal the sacramental test failed. The combination of bad harvests and religious restrictions further encouraged the emigration from Ulster to North America which had begun during the reign of Charles II. At the same time the more energetic and prosperous among both protestant and Catholic non-conformists began to apply their abilities with increasing success to various forms of trade and manufacture, thus laying the foundations of the Dissenting and Catholic middle classes, which developed steadily throughout the century and whose prosperity was greatly assisted by their overseas connections both with the Continent and with the American colonies.

On the political scene, although the Hanoverian succession was a national decision at least in England, the aura of Jacobitism which hung round the Tory politicians of the last years of Anne's reign guaranteed that it was also a Whig triumph. A similar political success was enjoyed by the former opposition politicians in Ireland. The recently appointed Tory Primate Lindsay was isolated and Archbishop King succeeded to the political rôle of Primate Marsh if not to his ecclesiastical dignity. Lord Chancellor Phipps resigned and Alan Broderick, created Baron Broderick in 1715 and Viscount Midleton two years later, succeeded to his office. Finally when the new parliament met in 1715 William Conolly was elected Speaker. In 1717 Archbishop King, Lord Chancellor Midleton and Mr Speaker Conolly were all appointed Lords Justices. However, the British ministers soon discovered that despite their Whig affiliations, and their undoubted devotion to the Hanoverian succession, Irish politicians inevitably regarded political issues from a Dublin rather than a London viewpoint.

One of the problems of governing a dependent country with the support of a locally elected legislature was that they looked to the Westminster parliament as a co-equal model and to its privileges as their rights, while the Westminster parliament was always anxious to point out its superior position as the imperial parliament and to emphasise that the king in parliament at Westminster was the final arbiter on all imperial issues. A situation which was essentially strengthened by the gradual alteration in the rôle of the British parliament emerged as a consequence of the Revolution Settlement and the Hanoverian succession. In the years following 1709 the series of appeals and contradictory verdicts in the Annesley-Sherlock case, which involved the inheritance to an estate, led to the declaration by the British parliament both of its right to legislate for Ireland and of its right to act as the final court of judicature for that country. This famous Declaratory Act of 1719, the 6th of George I, aroused all the latent sensibilities of the Irish parliament and the united disapproval of Archbishop King and Dean Swift.

Jonathan Swift, who for the next two decades was to be an irritant to successive governments, declared his own and the Irish parliament's opposition to the 1719 Declaratory Act in a vitriolic pamphlet advocating sanctions against English imports through an exclusive use of Irish goods, a theme which recurs in subsequent times of depression or political indignation. Swift was an individual whose tormented and complex personality has been the subject of much learned debate and controversy, but for this study it is perhaps sufficient to say that he was a man who combined strong convictions with a certain empiricism. He had hoped to make his career in England, but the Hanoverian succession obliged him to make it in Ireland; for instance, in 1711 he was writing to one of his correspondents, 'you are in the right as to my indifference to Irish affairs, which is not occasioned by my absence but contempt of them'. When he was appointed Dean of St Patrick's in 1713 Archbishop King remarked 'I thought a Dean could do less mischief than a Bishop'. Nevertheless, the verdict of history was to declare him an Irish patriot, and Archbishop King, after observing him as Dean for a decade, praised his services to the Irish Church as well as to the Irish state. It was hardly to be expected that the relationship between King and Swift would have been a smooth one; King was a stickler for the letter of the law and Swift was exceedingly touchy. Swift's prickly personality was further aggravated by his failure to gain the legitimate aspirations to which his abilities entitled him. He made the mistake of letting his contemporaries realise his brilliant intelligence and biting wit, and they reacted by distrusting him, perhaps because in addition he was a tormented person seldom, if ever, at ease with himself and this does not encourage confidence.

Swift's pamphlet in 1720 provoked the government into prosecuting the printer, in accordance with the usual eighteenth-century practice with anonymous publications – even when the authorship was an open secret. Despite repeated instructions from Lord Chief Justice Whitshed the jury refused to convict and only the arrival of the Lord Lieutenant, the Duke of Grafton, followed by a writ *nolle prosequi* brought the case to a close and restored a measure of public tranquillity. This tranquillity was short-lived. For some time the monetary circulation in the country had been hampered by a lack of small specie. The British ministry decided to remedy this situation and at the same time gratify the avarice of the king's mistress, the Duchess of Kendal. Accordingly the Duchess was granted a patent to issue a large quantity of copper coin which she sold to an iron-master called Wood.

However, this patent had been prepared without any previous consultation either with the Irish Privy Council or the Irish parliament, and it was far from clear that copper coinage was required to the exclusion of other varieties, as Archbishop King among others declared that: 'we have more halfpence than we need already. It is true we want change, but it is sixpences, shillings, half-crowns and crowns.' Thus two issues were involved: the utility of the coinage itself and the insult to the Irish parliament implicit in the lack of consultation as to its arrangement. Still smarting from the recent Declaratory Act, the reaction of parliament was predictable and the newly-appointed Primate Boulter (Primate Lindsay had died in 1723) informed Newcastle that: 'it is likewise certain that some foolish and other ill-meaning people, have taken this opportunity of propagating a notion of the independency of this kingdom on that of England . . . those of the best sense and estates here abhor any such notion . . . they esteem the greatest security of all they have here to lie on their dependency on the kingdom as well as the king of England.'

The country was inflamed by widespread propaganda to the effect that the coinage was defective and that they were about to be swindled by the English to please the king's German mistress and that tactless upstart, Wood. Swift took up the various aspects of the situation with his anonymous, but powerful, pen in the *Drapier's Letters*. The excitement increased rapidly to the alarm of both the Irish administration and the British government. In an attempt to control the situation, Lord Carteret was despatched to apply his 'perfect knowledge of men and things' to the pacification of the Irish parliament, while at the same time maintaining the prerogatives of English government. No less a person than Sir Isaac Newton, Master of the Mint, was requested to analyse the coinage and thereby convince the Irish populace, by force of scientific logic, that the coins were up to standard and that they were not being cheated. Nevertheless, public indignation had reached such a pitch that the only solution was to withdraw the patent and compensate both Wood and the Duchess of Kendal.

This solution and its implementation had required all of Carteret's diplomatic skills and political adroitness. To apply them he resided in the country constantly from October 1724 to April 1726. He was continued in office by George II and was recalled in 1730 having won 'great honour and reputation'. Few viceroys were so fortunate, or perhaps so skilful at giving satisfaction in both London and Dublin. Nevertheless, on Carteret's departure there lay beneath the ostensibly smooth surface of politics a groundswell of agitation on such subjects as absentees, the restrictions on the wool trade, the pension list and the stationing of Irish regiments abroad. When Carteret finally returned to England the building programme which was to make Dublin one of the most elegant cities in Europe had already begun; the great Jacobean Library of Trinity College was nearing completion, and the new Parliament House was under way.

Even today the memory of the Irish parliament still clings to the majestic pillared building in College Green. Built at the cost of £95,000, it was incomparably the most splendid Parliament House in the Empire, even eclipsing Westminster. The foundation stone of this magnificent edifice was laid in 1728, when Chichester House, once the property of James I's powerful Lord Deputy was demolished. The architect for the new Parliament House was Sir Edward Lovett Pearce, M.P. for Ratoath. Dying in 1733, Pearce did not live to see the completion of his great design, but its supervision was continued by another M.P., Arthur Dobbs, who sat for Carrickfergus and was later Governor of North Carolina. At that time he was Surveyor-General for Ireland, and under his direction the building was completed in 1739. It was built in the Italian style with a façade of Ionic columns, to which in 1785 James Gandon added the imposing pillared portico of the House of Lords. In 1776 Arthur Young commented that 'the appartments are spacious, elegant and convenient much beyond that heap of confusion at Westminster'; and some years later after making a similar comment John Wesley added, 'but what surprised me above all, were the kitchens of the House and the large apparatus for good eating. Tables were placed from one end of a large hall to the other; which, it seems, while the Parliament sits, are daily covered with meat at four or five o'clock for the accommodation of the members.' The scale of Irish hospitality was proverbial, and certainly at the end of the century it was customary for the Speaker to entertain the entire House of Commons and even some of the House of Lords at the time of the budget debates.

The Commons chamber was a circle, 51 feet in diameter, enclosed in a square. Wainscoted in Irish oak, the M.P.s' seats rose 15 feet in circular tiers to the gallery, where the students of nearby Trinity College across the Green could, along with fashionable Dublin society, listen to the speeches which towards the end of the century reached an exceedingly high standard. However, although aesthetically pleasing, the building was cold, and John Foster, the last Speaker, was particularly anxious to remedy this discomfort. In 1790 he was largely responsible for implementing a heating plan which resulted in the great fire of 1792. This gutted the chamber, but Foster's anxiety that M.P.s should retire in a dignified manner, even under these circumstances, nearly resulted in a number of bye-elections. Undeterred by the consequences of his previous plan, Foster subsequently took issue with the Italian architect employed to repair the damage, complaining that he had 'no idea of light or warmth but to exclude them'! The rebuilding, though similar to the original, failed to re-capture all of its splendour; but an even greater destruction was not far off, for a few years after the Union the entire Parliament House was sold to the Bank of Ireland for £40,000 on condition that the House of Commons should be altered beyond recognition. This was duly done in accordance with the plans of the Irish architect, Francis Johnston.

The House of Lords was situated to the right of the House of Commons, a wide rectangular room 30 feet wide by 40 feet long, with a semi-circular apse for the throne from which the Lord Lieutenant opened, prorogued and dissolved parliament in the name of his royal master, attired, until 1777, in the robes worn by King James II in 1689. The walls on either side were hung with tapestries commemor-ating the battle of the Boyne and the siege of Londonderry. Facing the throne at the far end of the chamber stood the Bar. Throughout the century the foundation of a noble family was increasingly the ultimate ambition of the vast majority of politicians, and the House of Lords enjoyed a respect and power unknown today. In 1789 Chief Secretary Hobart stated that 'the natural strength of the Irish parliament rests in the aristocracy'.

Archbishop King, Lord Midleton and Speaker Conolly all died between 1728 and 1729. In 1723 the almost forgotten Primate, Thomas Lindsay, had died. The careers of Lindsay's predecessor Narcissus Marsh and Archbishop King had shown the British administration the important rôle which an ecclesiastical statesman could exercise. Lindsay's obvious successor was Archbishop King, who had been passed over in 1713. King was now seventy-three years old and not in very good health, but perhaps more importantly in the eyes of the British ministers King represented the views of the Anglo-Irish; he had objected to the 6th of George I and had supported Swift in his demand for people to support Irish industry by dressing in clothes made from Irish materials, while his temperament was such that he was unlikely to prove the pliable administrator desired by the English ministers. 'He is very indiscreet', reported Lord Lieutenant Grafton in 1723, 'in his actions and expressions, pretty ungovernable, and has some wild notions which sometimes make him impracticable in business and he is, to a ridiculous extent national . . . He is very well affected to the King and an utter enemy to the Pretender and his cause. He is charitable, hospitable, a despiser of riches and an excellent bishop, for which reason he has generally the love of the country, and a great influence and sway over the clergy and bishops who are natives.'

Considering the situation, the British administration felt that, during the long absences of the Lord Lieutenant, a closer control over the government of Ireland was desirable. Therefore, they decided to appoint Hugh Boulter, Bishop of Bristol, to the Irish Primacy. On the resignation of Lord Midleton in 1725 another Englishman was sent over to occupy the chief legal position in Ireland. The Speaker alone was, and from the nature of his office remained, the choice of the Anglo-Irish gentry. Because government depended upon him for the management of the House of Commons he acted as a bridge between parliament and the administration; he was almost invariably one of the three Lords Justices, and the position was one of the greatest importance throughout the century. On Conolly's resignation, shortly before his death in 1729, Sir Ralph Gore was elected Speaker. Nevertheless, in the short time between his election and his death in 1733, Gore was having difficulty in taking over Conolly's position and the leadership of his party. The next Speaker, Henry Boyle, had better success and occupied the Chair for twenty-three years, undisturbed by any general election.

4 Economic Development during the Eighteenth Century

By the 1730s the foundations for the unprecedented prosperity which Ireland enjoyed in the late eighteenth century had been laid and they reflect the agrarian basis of Irish society. Great Britain was the natural outlet for Irish trade and this situation was confirmed by the mercantilist laws which controlled British imperial economic policy during the eighteenth century. Theoretically, mercantilism provided a unified system of imperial trade revolving round the mother country. It was established by a series of legislative checks and balances either passed by or at the instigation of the imperial government. These controlled the market by a mixture of prohibition and protection: goods which conflicted with the commercial interests of the mother country were in general prohibited, while those which complemented her economy, for example, West Indian sugar, Virginian tobacco and Irish linen were protected. In addition, the pre-eminent position of the mother country as the entrepôt of imperial trade was secured through a series of Navigation Acts. Ireland's trade was automatically part of this system.

The whole question of Great Britain's economic policy towards Ireland has been confused by an elaborate tangle of political ambition unsupported by economic realities, while proximity and connection has made comparisons both inevitable and in the circumstances peculiarly invidious. Ireland was and has remained an agrarian society. This basic fact has always circumscribed her wealth and her potential. No discoveries were made of mineral wealth in sufficient quantity to enable the whole country to participate to any major degree in the massive industrialisation which was such a feature of the British economy in the late eighteenth and nineteenth centuries. Thus Ireland's resources, unlike those of England, remained tied to her agricultural land; however, like England in the eighteenth century, Ireland's population expanded at first slowly but then with ever-increasing momentum from the 1770s until after the famine. Unfortunately Ireland required neither an additional labour force to meet the demands of industrialisation, nor an additional population to sustain.

On the whole, it is probable that mercantilism was worse in theory than in practice. Inevitably the apparent self-interest of this doctrine created among the dependencies of a vigorous and expanding nation both a complaint and an excuse. No European country in either the seventeenth or eighteenth centuries considered that the development of colonies was anything other than an investment designed for the benefit of the investor. By comparison with other European powers England's policy was not illiberal, especially as she always conceded, theoretically at least, that Englishmen or their descendants, though domiciled overseas, possessed the rights and liberties of Englishmen resident in England. This theory and the theory of mercantilism tended to come into collision over economic issues and the ensuing conflicts received a political expression which became more insistent during the course of the century. Nevertheless, both nature and design ensured that during the eighteenth century Ireland's principal trade would be with England and the value of Anglo-Irish imports and exports in pounds sterling expanded steadily between 1700 and 1800 rising from £427,603 to £4,862,626, and £372,585 to £3,482,691 respectively.

Although the goods imported greatly increased in volume throughout the century the merchandise which

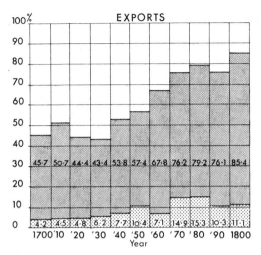

EXPORTS

	45·7	50·7	44·4	43·4	53·8	57·4	67·8	76·2	79·2	76·1	85·4
	4·2	4·5	4·8	6·2	7·7	10·4	7·1	14·9	15·3	10·3	11·1
1700	'10	'20	'30	'40	'50	'60	'70	'80	'90	1800

Year

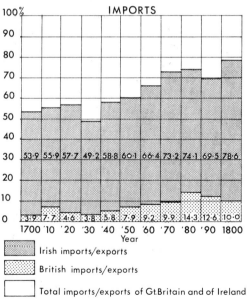

IMPORTS

	53·9	55·9	57·7	49·2	58·8	60·1	66·4	73·2	74·1	69·5	78·6
	3·9	7·7	4·6	3·8	5·8	7·9	9·2	9·9	14·3	12·6	10·0
1700	'10	'20	'30	'40	'50	'60	'70	'80	'90	1800

Year

Irish imports/exports

British imports/exports

Total imports/exports of Gt.Britain and of Ireland

The dominance of Great Britain in Irish trade.
Tables showing the approximate percentages of the import and export
trade between Great Britain and Ireland in relation to the total import
and export trade of both countries
(From the figures given in L. M. Cullen, *Anglo-Irish Trade 1660–1800*,
pp.46–7

Ireland imported from Great Britain varied considerably. The most stable demand was for coal, which accounted for between 6 per cent and 10 per cent of Ireland's imports from England and Scotland, and averaged over 8 per cent of her total imports from Great Britain throughout the century. The comparative share of other major imports fluctuated during the century. Among these commodities were muscovado sugar, which only accounted for 2.3 per cent of imports in 1698 and engrossed 13.7 per cent a century later; and tobacco, by far the largest single item in 1698 when it accounted for 26 per cent of all imports but by 1798 it had declined in comparative importance, though not in volume, to 5 per cent. From the 1730s onwards tea became an item of increasing importance; in 1718 it accounted for less than 2 per cent of Anglo-Irish trade but by 1788 the East India Company's monopoly in this sphere was accounting for nearly 13 per cent, although during the following decade its comparative position fell slightly to 10.5 per cent and at the close of the century only muscovado sugar, 13.7 per cent, and drapery, which at 23.6 per cent constituted by far the largest item in England's exports to Ireland, enjoyed a greater share of the import market most of which was made up by small imports of a wide range of goods.

Except in Dublin, where the volume of trade and the greater availability of capital encouraged a degree of specialisation, and in Cork, where the dominance of the provision trade made all other enterprises secondary to it, general rather than specialist merchants were the rule. Businesses were small and capital was difficult to accumulate, while modest returns were often further reduced by the need to reinvest in order to expand the enterprise. Thus in the middle of the century a prominent merchant, like Daniel Mussenden of Belfast, would invest a small stake in a number of enterprises: the diversification of Mussenden's interests included a wine company and a salt company, as well as linen and banking – for most Irish banks were originally merchant banks. His correspondents were widely scattered and his connections extensive, for instance, his London agents, Allen and Marlar, remitted and received funds from Mussenden's Dutch agents, Rocquette and Van Zeylingen of Rotterdam, who acted on his behalf as far away from Belfast as Trondheim and Danzig. Similarly the Frenchs of Galway were general merchants whose trading links can be traced to Bristol, France, Norway, Spain and Portugal.

Despite these complicated transactions the monetary economy of the country was for most of the century rudimentary. Although declining during the course of the century, barter was prevalent throughout Ireland and there were wide areas in which the value of money was probably very imperfectly understood. Apart from its simplicity, the continuance of this system was undoubtedly encouraged by the shortage of specie, which obtained to varying degrees throughout the century. In 1723–4 this scarcity had provoked the crisis which centred round Wood's halfpence. In addition, it often led to problems of currency and coinage which can only be described as indicative of financial chaos. There was no Irish mint. Coins were supposed to bear a direct relation to the value of their metal content, hence the severe penalties for counterfeiting or defacing them. The shortage of specie encouraged the circulation of all sorts of coins, particularly Spanish and Portuguese gold moidores. The value of these was fixed from time to time by proclamation, and merchants would carry small scales to weigh the coins they were handling. Nevertheless, the proclaimed value of these coins was often at variance with their real value. This upset the discounting system and encouraged speculators to play the Anglo-Irish money market, as for example, during the period 1717 to 1737, when the coinage was substantially composed of over-valued Portuguese gold moidores, and the silver coinage, which was undervalued, became extremely scarce. Finally a proclamation of 1737 adjusted the value of the moidores, and the $8\frac{1}{3}$ per cent discount between the English and the Irish pound was subsequently maintained until 1826, when the Irish currency was merged into that of the United Kingdom and the question of an exchange ceased. Throughout the century the currency of Great Britain's overseas possessions was discounted against the Bank of England £1 sterling.

This shortage of specie was a feature of mercantilism as was the centring of bills of exchange on London, and this, during periods of scarcity, could inflate their price in Ireland. A bill of exchange was the usual method whereby money was transferred from one place to another, and from one country to another. A merchant who sold goods at a distance would be in a position to draw a bill of exchange against his debtor. This bill could then be sold either to another merchant, or, perhaps, to an estate agent wishing to remit rents to an absentee landlord, or to anyone else who wished to transfer money to that place. When the bill of exchange was presented to the debtor he had to endorse it with his acknowledgement of the debt, and having done so to meet it, usually within twenty-one days. A bill of exchange was therefore a primitive type of cheque.

Banking was very unstable. Before the foundation of the Bank of Ireland in 1783 all Irish banks were private and appeared and disappeared with bewildering rapidity. The only bank which continued undisturbed by the vissicitudes of the century was the Dublin bank of the great Huguenot family of La Touche which enjoyed a considerable international reputation. The two major cities where banking of any size and continuity was conducted were Dublin and Cork, where the provision trade made foreign exchange essential, and the only inland town with any volume of banking was the Quaker town of Clonmel, a centre of the wool trade. Despite the prosperity of the linen trade there was no banking of any size or continuity in the North. The Ulsterman had a general distrust for any form of credit short of actual money and gold continued to be the basic form of circulation there until well into the nineteenth century. Consequently bills for linen sales were discounted in Dublin and the money was sent north to meet the direct cash transactions which were a feature of the linen markets. In 1783 the foundation of the Bank of Ireland, the country's first joint-stock bank, was a landmark in the development of Irish banking. Although nine-tenths of its capital was subscribed by Protestant and mainly landed interests, it is significant that the remaining capital was subscribed by Catholic business interests.

Information about the development of the Catholic urban middle class is difficult to acquire. During the penal period they were extremely reluctant to draw attention to themselves and in particular to their increasing prosperity. In the eighteenth century property not people was equated with political power, and the reformer Arthur Young pointed out that the Penal Laws 'actually do not seem to be so much levelled at the religion as at the property that is found in it'. This was important, for as the century progressed the accepted concept of property increasingly expanded to include first commercial wealth and then industrial capital. Nevertheless, by the reign of George III two factors are indicative of the increasing economic importance of this section of the community: firstly the relaxation of those parts of the Penal Code which prevented Catholics from investing their money in the economy of the country; and secondly, the reply of the Catholic Committee in 1792 to the accusation of inciting civil disturbance, when they declared that, 'they have a large stake in the country, much of it vested in that kind of property which is most peculiarly exposed to danger from popular tumult: THE GENERAL COMMITTEE WOULD SUFFER MORE BY ONE WEEK'S DISTURBANCES, THAN

ALL MEMBERS OF THE TWO HOUSES OF PAR-LIAMENT'. Considerable weight must adhere to this declaration when it is considered that Edward Byrne, the Chairman of the Catholic Committee in 1792, left an estate worth £400,000, and was reputed to be contributing £80,000 a year to the Irish exchequer in revenue duties during the 1790s. In the provincial towns, particularly of the south and west, trade was dominated by Catholic merchant houses like the Arthurs and, particularly, the Roches of Limerick. Dr William Drennan remarked in 1801 that the first physician, apothecary and merchant in Dublin were all Catholics. It can therefore be concluded that by the end of the century a fairly strong Catholic middle class had emerged, who possessed a very consider-able stake in the professional and commercial life of the country.

The graphs on p. 79 illustrate the relative position which Irish trade enjoyed in the total import/export trade of Great Britain and vice versa. Unlike the multiplicity of goods which Ireland imported, her exports remained few and remarkably stable throughout the century. For the first two decades wool, linen and provisions accounted for over 70 per cent and for the remainder they fluctuated between 80 per cent and 90 per cent. Some consideration of these three exports will indicate the nature of Ireland's commercial and industrial life.

The provision trade started the century under the mer-cantilist restrictions of the Cattle Acts passed by the English parliament in 1663 and 1666. These prohibited the export of live cattle to England and thus encouraged the decline of the smaller coastal ports like Galway, Youghal and Kinsale. This set-back was more than compensated for by the rise of the great provision trade and the consequent enlargement of Dublin, Cork, Limerick and Waterford as well as the inland market towns of Ballinasloe, Banagher and Mullingar. Eventually, in 1759, the restrictions on exporting live cattle into England were suspended, and finally, in 1776, they were repealed. Meanwhile, imperial expansion in the West Indies and the growing population in Great Britain were providing ready markets for Irish provisions. In addition, the recurrent wars of the century with their demand for military, and particularly naval, provisions provided a further outlet and one which was not confined to Great Britain alone, as French ships and French colonies were equally anxious to obtain these essential commodities. Between 1721 and 1741 the French mercantilist system was specifically altered to allow, under French law though not under the British mercantilist system, French ships to call to Cork on their way to the West Indies. In times of war these provisions were of vital strategic importance and the Irish government endeavoured to prevent provisions either being sold directly to French ships, or shipped for the same purpose to neutral European ports such as Stockholm, or to the great Dutch West Indian emporium of St Eustatia, which was so convenient for both the French West Indian fleet and the French islands, particularly Guadeloupe and Martinique. In March 1741 Lord Chancellor Jocelyn wrote to Lord Lieutenant Devonshire about rescinding the embargo placed on the export of beef and butter to Newfoundland, 'for fear of its falling into the hands of the French or by means of the Dutch be conveyed to them' as 'the stink and odious smell that came from the dock was enough to infect the whole country'.

By the middle of the century the Irish provision trade enjoyed a very favoured position both in peace and in war; a fact which was illustrated by the embargo placed on the export of provisions from 1776-9 by order of the Irish Privy Council on instructions from the British government. This caused a furore among the Irish parliamentary opposition, but their fulminations were not sustained by the scarcity implicit in the very high price which provisions were fetching during these years combined with the fact that in Cork alone the British government was spending upwards of half a million pounds sterling on the purchase of provisions. At the end of the century the French wars of the 1790s, and the ensuing Napoleonic wars, similarly gave an inflated prosperity to this aspect of the Irish economy. The provision trade made Cork very prosperous and indisputably the second city in Ireland with a population of about 80,000 by the end of the century. By the middle of the century it had built, or rebuilt, during the preceding forty years an Exchange, a Customs House, a new Cathedral and a Corn Market. The Mansion House was completed in 1767. The city often reminded travellers, like Arthur Young, of the Netherlands, as it had a net-work of canals and waterways, enabling goods to be brought in lighters to the merchants' warehouses. At the same time its dependence upon the provision trade made it the slaughter-house of Ireland. It has been estimated that some 300,000 head of cattle were slaughtered there each year, which must have created, even by eighteenth-century standards, a problem in municipal sanitation in contradistinction to the city's elegant walks and gardens.

The Irish cattle upon which the trade depended, were small, averaging 4–8 cwt. against the 10–15 cwt. of contemporary English breeds, features which possibly reflected their breed as well as the less advanced state of Irish agriculture, for although the agrarian revolution did make its impact in Ireland it came later than in England and Ireland had very much less capital to invest in it. Improvements were encouraged by the Dublin Society which from its foundation in 1733 stimulated and assisted agrarian reform. Among those who attempted to raise the standard of agriculture on their estates were the absentee Lords Shelburne and Hillsborough and the resident Earl of Shannon, John O'Neill, M.P. for County Antrim, and John Foster, M.P. for County Louth and last Speaker of the House of Commons. Residence did not always make a landlord virtuous, neither did absence inevitably make him a vicious oppressor of his unfortunate tenantry.

Arthur Young, who travelled in Ireland during the years 1776–9 considered that Irish agriculture was two hundred years behind that of England, and although this claim is probably excessive, nevertheless, some of the farming practices which he describes are both horrific and crude, for example 'they very commonly plough and harrow with their horses DRAWING BY THE TAIL'. Certainly this method saved the cost of harness and it was even argued that the horse preferred it! Other traditions were equally cruel, such as bleeding the cattle, plucking geese alive for their feathers, and parliament had actually passed an act forbidding the pulling wool off sheep by hand. At the same time an unscientific rotation of crops exhausted the soil, while inefficient methods of harvesting, for instance threshing corn with a flail and sieve, further reduced its produce.

The farming implements commonly in use were simple and basic. Flax was pulled by hand, grain was reaped with the sickle and hay cut with the scythe. A plough was made from a long wooden beam to which was added a metal sock. Those who possessed such a luxury often rented it to their neighbours at extortionate rates. The poorer people used a spade. In mountainous areas and on firmer bog-land, goods were carried on slide-carts, which were comparatively efficient on rough ground but so destructive to road surfaces that their use on highways was forbidden by Act of Parliament. The traditional vehicle was the Irish car which comprised two long shafts, solid wooden wheels and a wooden platform to which side-boards could be added for carrying grain or similar materials. By the end of the century the Scottish dray with its spoked wheels and iron axle was becoming popular, particularly in the North where it was used for transporting linen as well as for general farm purposes. Little care was taken of agricultural implements, which were frequently left out in the fields, as out-houses, where they existed at all, were usually inadequate. In general, Irish farms tended to be untidy, with poor fencing and badly hung gates or even none at all.

An over-simplified but common picture of Irish agrarian society during this century divides it into alien landlords oppressing wretched peasants. The reality was infinitely more complex, although the lack of social cohesion implicit in this idea is of particular importance: the eighteenth-century Irish landlord, in contradistinction to his English counterpart, failed to gain acceptance at the top of the agrarian social pyramid. Nevertheless, between the landlord and the cottier there were gradations of social strata varying from region to region, while beneath the cottier-tenant there were likewise gradations of casual labourer. The tendency towards subdivision intensified with the rise in population. The nature of this increase is shown by the graph on p. 14, and it was already causing concern to 'improving' landlords before the end of the century. Maria Edgeworth wrote of the period before 1782, that on her father's estate in County Longford, 'farms, originally sufficient for the comfortable maintenance of a man, his wife and family had, in many cases, been subdivided from generation to generation; the father giving a bit of land to each son to settle him . . . The maintenance was hardly sufficient to keep them one step above beggary; and insufficient even for this, when the number of their children increased. It was an absolute impossibility, that the land should ever be improved, if let in these miserable *lots*.'

One of the most unpopular figures on the Irish scene was the 'middle-man', described by Maria Edgeworth as 'taking land at a reasonable rent, and reletting it immediately to poor tenants at the highest price possible to be obtained from their necessities'. Although this situation was only too frequent, it was variable, as in some areas the middle men used their capital to encourage the development of dairy farming by leasing cattle along with land to prospective farmers who lacked the initial capital to provide their own stock. In any case this pernicious system was probably not as universal as has been previously believed, although middle-men tended to become entrenched in certain areas, particularly in the south-west where bad soil and poor communications made personal management difficult for the landlord of a large estate. Larger farms comprising upwards of 100 to 150 acres were usually found in the counties dominated by pasture lands such as Limerick, Clare, Tipperary, Roscommon, Meath and Waterford. The lessors of these farms formed, like the middle-men, a class of some affluence and frequently of considerable pretensions.

Nevertheless, the vast majority of the Irish population existed in the most primitive of housing, and on the most basic of diets. As the population rose the staple food became increasingly the potato, which gave a large return for a small amount of land. Inevitably the size of a potato patch or garden varied both in relation to its productivity and to the number it had to sustain, but on average it has been estimated that a poor family of six required 22 stones of potatoes a week and 170 stones for replanting the following year,—a total of 1,314 stones or 18,396 lb., and that this quantity of food could be grown annually on one, and the same, acre. Wherever possible the potato was supplemented by what was locally available, milk, butter-milk, a few vegetables, or on the coastal counties a little fish. The more prosperous peasant had some beef and bacon, while the greater prosperity and Scottish traditions of the North resulted in a diet which occasionally included meat, as well as porridge, milk, oaten-bread and garden vegetables. Despite the basic monotony of his diet, the Irish peasant was noted for his good physique, and many of the chair-men, coal-heavers and porters in London were Irishmen, while at the end of the century it was commented that the Irish soldiers in the British army were taller and stronger than their British counterparts.

Conditions and degrees of poverty varied from area to area. Income from poor land and small farms was often increased by additional earnings from weaving and spinning. Around the shores, particularly on the west coast and the offshore islands, subsistence agriculture was supplemented by fishing which in certain places formed another aspect of the provision trade. This was particularly true of the north-west where a flourishing fishing industry was built up in the latter half of the century, for instance in 1776 Mr Alexander, a Londonderry merchant, built a salting-house at Downings in County Donegal to prepare surplus herrings for the West Indian market, while further along the coast Mr Burton-Conyngham personally invested £30,000 and secured a parliamentary grant of £2,000 for development of the fisheries around his parliamentary borough of Killybegs. There was a large salmon fishery on the river Bann at Coleraine and nearby on Lough Neagh there were eel fisheries. The Bishop of Derry had a very large, and profitable, rabbit-warren at Magilligan, which in the 1770s was estimated to add at least £1,500 to his already large revenues. In County Dublin the proximity of the capital offered an encouragement to market gardening, and probably to a lesser degree the same was true of the area around Cork city.

Spinning of wool or linen, depending upon the area was almost universal throughout Ireland. Considerable efforts were made both by the government and by private individuals to encourage cottage industry, especially the linen manufacture, which despite attempts to introduce it throughout the country became concentrated in the North, particularly after the widespread recession which occurred in both Great Britain and Ireland during the early 1770s.

Much has been attributed to the part played by the Huguenot refugees in the development of the linen industry, especially to Louis Crommelin and the colony which he settled around Lisburn in 1698. Crommelin's arrival coincided with the British government's decision to encourage the already existent Irish linen industry and to restrict the woollen manufacture. The Irish administration, anxious to develop the linen industry, gave considerable financial aid to Crommelin's settlement at Lisburn, where a ready source of thrifty and hard-working labour was available in the surrounding counties. Crommelin's community was scattered by the great fire which destroyed the new settlement in 1707. Thereafter local rather than Huguenot names predominate in the manufacture. The particular skill of the Huguenots lay in producing fine linens, and in 1736 another Huguenot, de Joncourt, established a cambric manufactory at Dundalk. De Joncourt was encouraged in this enterprise by the Linen Board.

The Linen Board was established in 1711 to further the development of the industry. In this it was largely successful until it was disbanded in 1828. The encouragement it gave was along similar lines to the policy of the later Dublin Society, namely, it sponsored research and educational projects and gave prizes for various meritorious achievements. The Board was large, comprising 72 members, 18 from each of the 4 provinces, who were almost invariably members of one or other of the Houses of Parliament. Trusteeship of the Linen Board became a much sought-after honour, and, although this political link was valuable in the Board's early years, it tended ultimately to make it honourable but moribund. The conduct of its business came increasingly into the hands of its permanent officials, and as the manufacture expanded the merchants involved found that the Board had outstripped its usefulness. The linen manufacture involved the whole family, the women and children spinning the yarn and the men weaving and marketing the cloth. A skilled weaver could absorb the work of a number of spinners, consequently there was a considerable amount of spinning in the counties surrounding Ulster, such as Sligo where Arthur Young observed that in the 1770s 'the rents are mostly paid by yarn'. This was even more the case in the major weaving counties like Antrim and Down.

Merchandising linen required capital and credit and, because of the finance involved, Dublin was for most of the century the centre of the linen export. The finished white linens were brought from all over Ireland for sale at the Dublin Linen Hall, the streets around which were appropriately named after the northern linen towns, Lisburn Street, Lurgan Street and Coleraine Street. Other important linen towns were Londonderry, Banbridge, Dundalk and Belfast where a Linen Hall was finally established in 1785. The webs which were woven in the cottages were sold by the weavers at the local fairs as brown linen. The linen drapers who bought the webs were either bleachers themselves, or bleachers' agents. As the century progressed, the markets became more specialised and centred on the larger towns like Banbridge, Lurgan or Ballymoney. This encouraged the development of a class of middlemen who bought webs in outlying districts and resold them at the major fairs. Once the cloth was bought, it was bleached and the impurities removed on the bleachers' bleach greens. Prior to 1785 the finished white linen was then taken to the Linen Hall in Dublin. After this date much of the northern linen was channelled through the new Linen Hall in Belfast.

However, by 1785 Linen Halls were already outmoded, as many of the manufacturers had by then amassed sufficient capital to trade directly with the English merchants, for, by the second half of the century, the bleachers were not only prosperous but even wealthy. For instance, when the Quaker manufacturer Thomas Christie of Moyallen

£100,000 and over

COLERAINE

L/DERRY

Londonderry
£260,000

Antrim
£400,000

BELFAST

Donegal
£80,000

U L S T E R

KILLYBEGS

Tyrone
£100,000

Down
£400,000

Fermanagh
£15,000

Armagh
£280,000

NEWRY

Monaghan
£60,000

Sligo
£27,000

Leitrim
£5,000

Cavan
£50,000

Louth
£100,000

DROGHEDA

Mayo
£10,000

Roscommon
£20,000

Longford
£20,000

Meath
£40,000

C O N N A C H T

Westmeath
£40,000

Dublin

DUBLIN

Galway
£40,000

L E I N S T E R £100,000

GALWAY

BALLINASLOE

Kings County
£60,000

Kildare
£20,000

Wicklow
£200

Queens County
£300

Clare
£1,000

Carlow
£500

Kilkenny

LIMERICK

Tipperary
£100

Wexford
£300

Limerick
£1,000

£6,000

CLONMEL

WATERFORD

M U N S T E R

Waterford

Kerry
£400

Cork
£10,000

CORK

A map showing the distribution of sales of linen cloth in 1770 (From
the report prepared by Robert Stephenson for the House of Commons
and the Trustees of the Linen manufacture)

died in 1780, he left £2,000 to each of his five grand-daughters, while his two grandsons inherited in addition to various moneys the 6,000 acres of land which he owned in North Carolina; finally the core of his estate, the large bleach green and a considerable amount of property scattered throughout Ulster was left to their father, his son-in-law. To another son-in-law and his children he also left considerable legacies. Capital on this scale eventually turned the Irish linen manufacture from a cottage into a factory industry in the nineteenth century. During the eighteenth century Ireland was relatively but not completely unaffected by the industrial revolution, as is illustrated by the development of the factory-based cotton industry which started around 1750. Encouraged by the Linen Board, it had established itself in Counties Dublin, Kildare, Meath, Carlow, Waterford and Cork before 1782. In 1785 the Irish parliament voted £96,000 to further its growth, and this was used to purchase spinning jennies and copy the use of water-power developed in England during the preceding decades. In the 1780s spinning factories began to appear in a number of towns, and from 1790 to 1830 the cotton industry was particularly flourishing in Belfast where its expansion almost annihilated the linen manufacture, as between 1760 and 1810 the number of linen looms in the town decreased from 400 to 4 while the number of cotton looms rose from none to 860. The industry received its initial support from the Belfast Charitable Society which wished to provide a trade for the children under its care.

Among other symptoms of Ireland's awareness of the industrial revolution was the limited use of the steam engine, the first of which had been introduced into the country about 1740. By the end of the century one Dublin merchant had three in use: one in a foundry, one for rolling and slitting iron and a third to power a grinding wheel.

Between 1770 and 1814 large mills began to appear throughout the country. The most famous of the early mills was the water-powered flour mill at Slane built between 1763 and 1767 at a cost of £20,000. Mills like this altered the economic pattern of everyday life in the country, though whereas the traditional mills had ground flour on commission, and in small towns the local baker had often kept his supplies in a locked chest at the mill to be ground on request, the new large mills bought the grain outright and then sold the finished product on the open market. Nevertheless, lack of capital and basic raw materials largely inhibited Ireland's participation in the industrialisation which by the end of the century was becoming increasingly prevalent in Great Britain.

Ireland's third major export was woollen yarn. Although the mercantilist policies of the British government cannot be said to have injured the provision trade, and certainly encouraged the linen manufacture, their effect on the woollen industry is less clear-cut. The principal cloth made at the end of the seventeenth century was frieze, a coarse woollen cloth which was woven throughout the country. Organised as a cottage industry, it principally supplied the home market and it continued to do so throughout the eighteenth century. The English prohibition applied to exports abroad, mainly to Europe. Exports to England were not legally forbidden but effectively prohibited by high duties, while from 1799 the number of ports, from which and to which woollen products could be exported, were restricted by law. Undoubtedly the attitude of the English parliament to the Irish woollen industry shows the petty and irritating aspects of the mercantilist system, but its ultimate effect on the development of the industry is speculative for, given the capital and the expertise of the long-established English industry and finally the unforeseeable industrialisation of the later eighteenth century, it is improbable that the weaker Irish industry would have survived against British capital and English competition on an open market.

During the eighteenth century the woollen industry was largely centred in the South of Ireland and it was dominated by the Quakers. 'The poor Catholics in the south of Ireland spin wool very generally', wrote Arthur Young in the 1770s, 'but the purchase of their labour, and the whole worsted trade is in the hands of the Quakers of Clonmel, Carrick, Bandon, &c.' The Quakers played a very considerable part in many aspects of the Irish economy in the eighteenth century. They and the Presbyterians often had business as well as social connections with their co-religionists in the North American colonies, while many Catholic merchants had similar connections with the continent. Not all of these connections were strictly legal as the various illegalities of many aspects of life during the penal era, and the rigidity of the mercantilist system, encouraged other clandestine activities such as smuggling. Early in the century wool had been one of the commodities smuggled from the West coast to the continent but from the 1730s onwards the expanding English woollen industries, particularly those of Lancashire, Yorkshire and East Anglia, were anxious to acquire Irish yarn as the low cost of labour, despite the cost of freight, made it comparatively cheaper than any other source of supply. In 1739 pressure from these manufacturing interests prevailed upon the British parliament to remove the duties on woollen and worsted yarn. Similar pressures in 1752 and 1753 opened ports previously closed to Irish woollen imports which had been confined to Exeter and various ports on the West coast of England. Thus in accordance with mercantilist principles, the Irish woollen exports had become complementary to the English woollen manufacture. Whether it would have done better in competition, or whether a free trade would not have led to this situation anyway, is a matter for speculation. The mercantilist system simply ensured that its rôle became complementary rather than competitive, and in return protected the linen industry from foreign rivals, encouraging its development by guaranteeing it an expanding market in Great Britain and her colonies.

In conclusion some mention should perhaps be made of smuggling, an activity which mercantilism inevitably encouraged by its prohibitions, and although from time to time during the century there was some variation in both the goods and quantities in demand, the three principal commodities in this illicit market remained spirits, tobacco and tea. The best profits for smugglers lay in the east of Ireland and in particular in the area around Dublin. Until 1765, when it was acquired by the British government for £70,000, the great smuggling entrepôt in the Irish sea was the Isle of Man. The Isle of Man was an independent possession of the Duke of Athol and levied its own extremely low customs duties to encourage this entrepôt smuggling trade. In 1765, when this came to an end, direct trade with the Continent was resumed, although the island of Guernsey partly inherited the Isle of Man's position. In Ireland the small port of Rush in County Dublin became the most notable haunt of the professional smuggler, whose main imports were high duty commodities, and whose various exports included such unexpected articles as counterfeit money and pirated editions of books, for the law of copyright did not apply to Ireland. Often the smugglers used well-equipped, fast, armed vessels and in war-time these entrepreneurs often became French privateers. Among the more notorious examples of this were two ships called the *Black Prince* and the *Black Princess,* both manned by smugglers from Rush. During the American war they made considerable depredations off the Irish coast.

The variation in the type of smuggler was immense and many generally legitimate traders undoubtedly also engaged in a little smuggling. For instance the Belfast merchant, John Black, who had many interests and was blessed with many sons, wrote in 1766 to two of them in London, Alexander and James, that Tom and Sam were busy either at the bleach-green or arranging for their brother Robert's arrival when he should wind up his business at Douglas, Isle of Man, – the family had a firm in Bordeaux from which brandies had been consigned to the firm of Ross, Black and Christian on the Isle of Man. This mixture of legitimate and illegitimate trading undoubtedly complicated the work of the revenue officials, many of whom were poorly qualified and worse paid for the duties expected of them. Eighteenth-century administration in all its aspects was exceedingly lax by twentieth-century standards, and this was particularly the case with the customs and excise officials, to whom the strict enforcement of mercantilist policies presented an almost impossible task. For example one entry in the eighteenth-century account books of the O'Connells of Kerry reads: 'To ——, the boatman who came here seeking a prey 5s. 5d.' The O'Connells were noted smugglers, as one of them later recorded 'their faith, their education, their wine and their clothing were equally contraband'. Nevertheless, while smuggling was undoubtedly a problem, it is possibly debatable whether it existed either to the degree alleged, or whether it was worse in Ireland than it was in any other British possession. The nature of this activity makes it difficult both to acquire sufficient evidence or to evaluate correctly what evidence exists.

5 The Age of the 'Undertakers', c. 1730–1767

IN 1730, having proved his political skill in a difficult office during a period of particular tension, Lord Carteret returned to pursue his political career in Great Britain. He was succeeded by the Duke of Dorset, viceroy from 1730 to 1736. Dorset's administration was uneventful, apart from an unsuccessful movement in 1733 to repeal the 1704 sacramental test as it affected the protestant dissenters. In December 1731 Sir Robert Walpole had written to the Duke of Dorset commenting that: 'the time seems not only very favourable . . . it is represented to us that the House of Lords will be very desirous of passing such a Bill, that in the House of Commons the opposition will be much less than was ever apprehended . . . and I shall be glad that your Grace may have the honour of passing a Bill to relieve the protestant dissenters from a burthen which they have a long time unjustly and unreasonably groaned under.' However, contrary to Walpole's expectation, the House of Commons remained rigidly opposed to any such concession: 'I am apt to think', Archbishop Boulter informed Newcastle in December 1733, 'that there were near three to two against it . . . I hear some among the Dissenters, especially among their ministers, are very angry on this occasion.' The feeling in parliament was obviously so strongly against repealing the test that in the end the government decided not to introduce the motion into the House of Commons.

The most notable feature of the legislation which came

onto the statute book during these years was the number of bills for improving the roads, especially by building turnpikes. The need for better communications was an indication of the growing economic and commercial development which began about this period and which gained momentum as the century progressed. Another improvement in communications which dates from the 1730s was the building of canals; a project which received not only considerable but continuing support from the Irish parliament. It came to represent the most capital-intensive industrial investment undertaken in Ireland during the century: although it is probable that the system as a whole did not fully justify this investment. The Newry canal was financially the most successful. This canal was also the earliest, being built between 1731 and 1742 to link Newry on Carlingford Lough with the inland Lough Neagh and the Tyrone coalfield which it was hoped would develop. This expectation proved illusionary; nevertheless, Newry flourished, but on Irish linen not on Irish coal.

In 1730 the Irish parliament appointed Commissioners of Navigation for each of the four provinces, and at the same time the proceeds of certain duties were set aside for canal building. These arrangements were modified in 1751 when the Commissioners of Navigation were merged into the Corporation for Promoting and Carrying out an Inland Navigation, usually known as the Board of Inland Navigation. Its major scheme was the Grand Canal, which through its southern and western branches linked Dublin with Waterford *via* the Barrow river system and with Limerick *via* Ballinasloe and the river Shannon. This scheme was barely completed by the end of the century. The other major scheme was the Royal Canal. This canal was started in 1789 and completed in 1817. It ran westward in a northern parallel to the Grand Canal. The improvement of inland communications was always sure of strong support from the Irish gentry, not only through parliamentary grants of public money, but also by personal investment. They subscribed large sums to the turnpike trusts which built and maintained the roads with varying degrees of success during the period 1730 to 1760, and afterwards to the companies involved in building canals.

By the 1730s stage-coaches were operating regular services from Dublin to Cork, Drogheda and Kilkenny. Gradually these services were expanded northward to Newry, and on 13 August 1752, the first stage-coach set out from Dublin to Belfast. It was drawn by six horses, and the journey of just over 100 miles took three days. A regular service between Belfast and Dublin was not established until 1788. Similarly the service was extended westward to Athlone, and by the final decade of the century most areas of importance had been brought into the network of coach routes operating throughout the country. A stage-coach, at the end of the century, carried ten people inside and rather more on top. The amount of luggage allowed the passengers was strictly limited, and anything above 20 lb. was liable to be surcharged for the excess – if not actually refused. In 1810 the journey from Dublin to Drogheda, approximately 30 miles, cost 6s. 6d. outside and 8s. 8d. inside.

Most travellers throughout the century commented favourably on the state of the Irish roads, although, as they were composed of stones of varying sizes embedded in earth, it was probably easier to ride than to travel in a carriage. Certainly for most of the century the Irish Bar on circuit rode with their briefs in their saddle-bags followed by mounted servants carrying their books and gowns. In this way considerable distances could be covered; in 1750 John Wesley, riding near Kilkenny, wrote: 'I think this was the longest day's journey I ever rode; being fifty of Irish, that is, about ninety English miles' – an Irish mile was 480 yards longer than an English one. However, nearly forty years later in 1787 the evangelist, now eighty-four years of age, declared indignantly that 'we went through horrible roads to Newry. I wonder that any should be so stupid as to prefer Irish roads to the English. The huge unbroken stones, of which they are generally made, are enough to break any carriage in pieces.' Some roads were undoubtedly better than others. Also, Irish roads did not always follow a logical pattern as many of the county gentry, who composed the Grand Juries, were not opposed to building roads to their houses, which resulted in a crisscross of roads throughout the country, and they also disliked having roads running across their property, which resulted in some peculiar bends and twists. In 1759 an Act of parliament attempted to have the roads between market towns made straight and of a certain width, but, as the application of the statute depended upon the Grand Jury of the county or counties concerned, the success of this measure was limited. Following the establishment of the Irish Post Office, which was separated from that of Great Britain in 1784, the Postmaster-General was given authority to widen and strengthen old roads, and where necessary create new ones, to carry the mail and these were paid for by the central government.

From the reign of James I a general charge for roadbuilding had been laid on each parish, which also supplied the necessary labour and equipment. The 1759 Act abolished this compulsory labour, which had always been unpopular and was almost invariably inefficient. From this date roads became a charge on the county rate or cess, a tax which fell largely upon the tenants and which financed all the administrative activities of the Grand Juries. That the gentlemen of the Grand Juries were not adverse to using their influence for their convenience and to provide jobs for their friends is indicated by Swift's devastating couplet on the construction of a bridge near Lucan in County Dublin which was erected under the auspices of the local landlord, Agmondisham Vesey:

'Agmondisham Vesey, out of his bounty,
Built a fine bridge – at the expense of the county.'

Recalled in 1736 the Duke of Dorset was succeeded by another great peer, the 3rd Duke of Devonshire, who held office from 1737 to 1744 Devonshire was a munificent supporter of public works and he built a quay to further the development of Irish trade. However, shortage of specie had resulted in the circulation of foreign coins, particularly gold moidores, which had become overvalued to the detriment of commercial intercourse. The revaluation of foreign gold was done by proclamation in 1737. This was strongly opposed by the bankers and remitters who suffered in the short-term from the lowering of the value of these gold coins. Under these circumstances this proclamation created a certain amount of opposition during Devonshire's first parliamentary session and on the day on which the proclamation came into force Dean Swift had a black flag hoisted on St Patrick's Cathedral and tolled the passing-bell! The city of Cork ordered its members to oppose the Money Bill; the viceroy, however, refused to be ruffled and the bill passed with a comfortable majority.

During these years the Irish parliament's uneasy fears were once again aroused when Lord Clancarty, who was a British naval officer and Governor of Newfoundland from 1733-5, endeavoured to persuade the British cabinet in 1736 to consider sponsoring a bill to reverse his father's attainder and restore his family estates which had an income estimated at £60,000 a year. 'I can assure your Lordship any thing of this nature will be a great blow to the Protestant interest here, and will very much shake the security Protestants think they now have of the enjoyment of their estates under his Majesty and his Royal family . . . and', Archbishop Boulter emphasised to Newcastle, 'I think the affair of the last importance to the Protestant interest here, which makes me take the liberty to lay the case before you.' Archbishop Boulter's warning and the immediate reaction of the Irish parliament brought the implications of such a concession before the British government and Clancarty's appeal was rejected. Subsequently Clancarty left to join the

Jacobites in France. He was implicated in the '45 Rebellion and he died in exile in 1769.

However, the dominant event of Devonshire's vice-royalty was the terrible famine of 1739–40. This was the worst natural disaster of the century and the subsequent pestilence, a typhus-type infection, decimated the debilitated population. Typhus fever and smallpox were both endemic in the country. From time to time throughout the century, but with greater frequency during the first half, these diseases flared to epidemic proportions. In 1734 Dr Rogers, a Cork physician, estimated that two in every eleven cases of smallpox were fatal. Although inoculation was known it is difficult to calculate its effect as both the extent of its application and the consequences of its practice are unknown. Before the advent of vaccination, which was not widely practised until the nineteenth century, inoculation might save an individual but by introducing the infection wreak havoc in a community. Tuberculosis, bronchial and rheumatic complaints were widespread. Diseases which were encouraged by the notorious Irish weather.

To convince himself that Ireland really had a higher rainfall than England the methodical Arthur Young kept a register from 20 June to 20 October 1776: 'and', he writes, 'there were in 122 days 75 of rain and very many of them incessant and heavy'. Two years later on 24 June 1778 Wesley complained that 'for exactly two months, we have had only two days without rain'. Both Wesley and Young were referring to the Irish summer and undoubtedly the all-pervasive damp and cold were among the major unpleasantnesses of Irish life. Efforts to mitigate them, by stopping up the windows and chimneys of cabins which possessed such refinements, ruined the women's complexions and scorched their legs, while smoke increased the instance of eye diseases.

Scientific medicine was still in its infancy. Old Celtic

families had their hereditary physicians whose traditional remedies were handed down from father to son, but folk medicine depended largely upon charms and superstitions, some of which like those for warts and ringworm continue until this day. Then, as now, various theories were held about the particular virtues of certain foods. John Wesley speaks of his concern about finding a 'young preacher in a deep consumption; from which, I judge, nothing can recover him, unless perhaps a total butter-milk diet'. Often when Wesley had finished giving spiritual advice he endeavoured to give medical assistance, and he was extremely scathing about the various medical fashions which were current from time to time. 'I generally asked', he recorded, '"What remedies have you used?" and was not a little surprised . . . Blisters, for anything or nothing, were all the fashion when I was in Ireland last. Now the grand fashionable medicine for twenty diseases (who would imagine it?) is mercury sublimate! Why is it not a halter, or a pistol? They would cure *a little* more speedily.' Another curious remedy was that advocated by the distinguished philosopher George Berkeley, Bishop of Cloyne. Concerned by the terrible distress around him in the early 1740s Berkeley advocated tar-water as a panacea.

It is extremely difficult to assess the effects of the developments in social and medical care during the century. Only a very small section of the population was affected by the enthusiastic efforts of devoted individuals to alleviate the misery which was so prevalent around them. The Elizabethan Poor Law had made the English poor the responsibility of the parish in which they resided, but this law, and its subsequent modifications, did not apply to Ireland where the problems which it attempted to mitigate were much greater. In 1703 the Irish parliament established a Workhouse in Dublin and during the century many of the larger towns erected similar 'Houses of Industry' some of which had hospital accommodation. An Act of 1787 empowered the Grand Juries to present the sums necessary for establishing wards for lunatics, but it was generally ignored, although the Houses of Industry at Dublin, Cork, Limerick and Waterford provided accommodation for about 200 of the mentally ill poor. Nevertheless, this provision, like all hospital accommodation during the eighteenth century, was quite inadequate, and those who were turned away either roamed the country, found their way into prisons or were cared for at home.

Towards the end of the century the dispensary movement marked a new development in medical care. It found its impetus partly in private subscriptions and partly in legislative action, and the exact origin of most dispensaries is unknown. Like the hospitals, the dispensaries were too few in number to perform the service required of them. In addition they were unevenly distributed, being fairly numerous in Leinster and virtually unknown in the more remote areas of Connacht. Their work was also hampered by lack of adequate funds.

The eighteenth century was not insensible to these problems, but the organisation, resources and knowledge required to give them an adequate solution were not available until the nineteenth or even the twentieth century. Nevertheless, the number of Dublin hospitals which were founded in the eighteenth century, indicate that this was a period of expansion and development both in medical care and in the provision of hospitals. Some of these hospitals received spasmodic parliamentary grants, but all depended essentially upon voluntary subscriptions or charitable fundraising activities. Where Dublin led, the rest of the country followed and by the end of the century almost every county had its infirmary, although the facilities and accommodation were totally inadequate to the need. As with the Dublin hospitals, those throughout the country were largely the result of private enterprise and public subscription. Parliament did recognise the situation in an Act of 1765, which made the clergy of the established Church a perpetual corporation for the erection of infirmaries, fixed the qualification for governors by subscription, and empowered grand juries to make presentments or grants of up to £100.

At the beginning of the century the only known hospitals were military ones. Over one-third of the 10,000 troops which the Marshal Duke of Schomberg disembarked in 1689 were alleged to have died in one such hospital in Belfast. The only late seventeenth-century hospital about which there is any detailed knowledge is the Royal Hospital of Charles II, built at Kilmainham in 1670, for the relief and maintenance of ancient and maimed officers and soldiers of the army in Ireland – an Irish counterpart of the Chelsea Hospital. The first known civilian hospital in Ireland was opened in Dublin in 1726 and contained four beds. Then in 1733 under the will of Dr Steevens, who had died in 1717, Steevens Hospital was established and provided forty beds for poor patients to be chosen without distinction of religion or ailment so long as the latter was not infectious. Interest in building and endowing new hospitals, both in the capital and throughout the country, increased with each decade. Many of these hospitals received considerable support from social events held for charitable purposes. Possibly the best example of this is the Lying-in Hospital, better known as the Rotunda – taking its name from the Assembly Rooms which were its most constant support. Enlarged in 1785, the Rotunda became the social centre of Dublin, and the engraver Malton declared during the last decade of the century: 'that the entertainments of the Rotunda during the winter form the most elegant amusements of Dublin; it is open every Sunday evening in summer, for the purpose of a promenade, when tea and coffee are given in the superb upper room. The receipts of the whole after defraying incidental expenses go to the support of the hospital.' This famous hospital, the first maternity hospital in the British Isles, was founded in 1745 by Dr Bartholomew Mosse. During the preceding year the Charitable Musical Society had opened a hospital for incurables. It was this society which in 1742 sponsored the first performance of Handel's *Messiah* given when the famous composer visited Dublin in response to the viceregal invitation of the Duke of Devonshire. In the course of his visit Handel also gave a benefit concert for Mercer's Hospital, founded by Mrs Mary Mercer in 1734.

Devonshire's viceroyalty saw the formation of a close link between the Cavendish and Ponsonby families: in the course of it two of his daughters married two sons of Brabazon Ponsonby, Lord Duncannon, who was created Earl of Bessborough in 1739. This connection was of significance for the development of Irish political alignments during the latter part of the century. Brabazon Ponsonby was originally part of Speaker Conolly's political group. After Conolly's death he led one of the remnants of his party. During the 1730s he gradually consolidated his position, until following these marriages he emerged as a major political figure. In 1739 Brabazon Ponsonby, now Earl of Bessborough, succeeded Henry Boyle as first commissioner of the revenue, and three years later he resigned this position to his younger son, John Ponsonby. Thus from about 1740 the Ponsonby family emerges as a leading influence in Irish politics, drawing strength both from their Irish background and their English connections. Nevertheless, despite these family alliances, Devonshire, from a position of lofty eminence, remained impartial, but the power block which his alliances created carried with it the virtual certainty of trouble for his successors.

In 1739 England went to war for the first time since the Hanoverian succession. By 1740 Great Britain was involved in the general European war, which followed the succession of the Archduchess Maria Theresa to the Austro-Hungarian possessions of her father, the Emperor Charles

VI. The War of Austrian Succession lasted from 1740 to the Peace of Aix-la-Chapelle in 1748. Ireland, decimated by famine during the early years of the war, remained quiet and loyal throughout. The able and liberal Earl of Chesterfield succeeded the Duke of Devonshire in 1745. It was during his short viceroyalty that, encouraged by the French, the Stuarts represented by Prince Charles Edward, made their last attempt to recover their ancestral possessions in the great Scottish rebellion of 1745–6. Set against the background of a major European war this rebellion at first met with unexpected success. The Jacobite forces reached Derby before their over-extended lines made their retreat northward advisable, and it was in Scotland that the King's favourite son, the Duke of Cumberland, finally defeated them at Culloden Moor on 16 April 1746.

Chesterfield refused to be panicked by the Scottish Rebellion and endeavoured to point out that the country should be as watchful 'against poverty as against popery'. The custom of closing Catholic churches in times of crisis led to unsuitable buildings being used for worship. In 1744 this had resulted in the death of ten worshippers and the injury of many more when a floor in one such building collapsed. Subsequently, with the viceroy's encouragement, official permission was obtained to open Catholic churches and thereby prevent a repetition of such a disaster. Concerned for the economic development of the country, and appalled by its poverty, which visitors continually commented upon, Chesterfield supported the Dublin Society's plans for the improvement of commerce and agriculture, while he encouraged the nobility and gentry to wear clothes made from Irish materials at official receptions. Military affairs inevitably occupied much of Chesterfield's period of office, and he tried to substitute Admiralty contracts for provisions as compensation for the wartime embargoes placed on Irish exports.

The politically-powerful Primate Boulter, upon whom

Walpole and his ministers had depended for eighteen years, died in 1742. Archbishop Hoadly, who had been Archbishop of Dublin since the death of Archbishop King in 1729, was appointed to succeed him. Before Hoadly had fully established his position he died in 1747 and his place was filled by George Stone, Bishop of Derry and younger brother of Newcastle's confidential secretary, Andrew Stone. The Pelham brothers were the most pervasive element in British politics between the fall of Walpole in 1742 and the death of Henry Pelham in 1754, and some indication of the importance of Andrew Stone's position can be gauged from the fact that on one occasion Newcastle wrote to his brother, Henry Pelham, 'whatever you order me not to communicate, I never will but to *Stone* who knows everything'. George Stone's appointment to the Primacy was among the first acts of Lord Chesterfield's successor, the Earl of Harrington. Boulter had been fifty-two at the time of his appointment in 1724 and Hoadly sixty-eight when he succeeded him in 1742. Stone was probably under forty at the time of his elevation in 1747; the rapidity of his ecclesiastical advancement can only be ascribed to the strength of his connections in England and to the desire of the British administration to place this important appointment in safe hands.

Some assessment of the character of Archbishop Stone, 'the never-to-be-forgotten political primate' is important in view of subsequent events. Stone emerges from his letters as an expedient politician who liked power and enjoyed the exercise of it almost as an end in itself; he lacked the ballast and judgement of a statesman. As a person he had great social gifts and considerable charm of manner, which he exerted so widely that its impact lost sincerity when he most needed to convey this quality. Essentially he was more suited to the shallows of political manipulation than to the ocean of insoluble problems on which he was now called to embark. Consequently he laid himself open to the vicious and groundless attacks of the opposition press, whose mud has stuck to a man whose principal fault was a mixture of mediocrity combined with his adherence to a type of political expediency which undermined the confidence of his associates. It is not improbable that Stone simply envisaged his rôle as that of Archbishop Boulter's successor, the great ecclesiastical servant of the Crown in Ireland, and perhaps it was his misfortune that he lacked the character, skill and judgement for the rôle he envisaged in the extraordinarily difficult situation which speedily developed around him.

An anti-establishment press had gradually emerged during the 1740s. This political journalism gained an increasing momentum throughout the viceroyalty of Lord Chesterfield's less able successor, the Earl of Harrington. Prior to his arrival in Ireland Lord Harrington had incurred the displeasure of George II, whose views were always of paramount importance to his ministers, and this undoubtedly increased the Lord Lieutenant's nervous anxiety, which inevitably encouraged the opponents of his government to increase his difficulties. On his arrival Harrington was confronted with the demands of Dr Charles Lucas, a Dublin apothecary and journalist of considerable force and vituperative power. Lucas brought forward a series of charges against the electoral policy of the city of Dublin, parliament and the judiciary. He expressed and extended the views of Molyneux and Swift, and what his arguments lacked in intellect and style, he remedied in the strength and violence of his expression.

Although less self-seeking, Lucas possessed many of the exhibitionist characteristics, and much of the same type of irritation for the Irish government that John Wilkes was to provide for the British ministers during the early reign of George III. Finally he goaded the government to such a degree that in 1749 the exasperated viceroy declared that 'it is become absolutely necessary to put an immediate stop to his proceedings' and, with the assistance of the 'under-takers' the administration persuaded the House of Commons to pass a series of resolutions declaring Lucas a public enemy and ordering his immediate arrest. Lucas, who was popular with the Dublin guilds, though in no sense a friend to the Catholics, was forced to go into exile for some years, having to some extent been made a popular martyr.

Thus the government's action became increasingly unpopular and as this became evident the Lord Lieutenant's supporters, who had included the Ponsonbys, retired leaving the opprobrium firmly attached to the viceroy and the new Primate, Archbishop Stone. Lucas was not the only problem confronting Harrington. His other major hazard was less obvious and more dangerous. On his arrival Lord Harrington found that the Irish treasury was in an unusually prosperous condition. A situation 'which had arisen partly from a saving made in consequence of the low Establishment before the peace, and partly from an extraordinary importation of several kinds of commodities since the conclusion of it, being by . . . [all his advisors] . . . judged sufficient with the growing produce of the revenue to bear the whole charge of the Establishment, Civil and Military, for the two years to come at least'. Under these circumstances Harrington decided to request only 'the usual supplies' from parliament and not to make any additional request for further supplies. However, when the Money Bills were sent over, the Lord Lieutenant wrote to his official correspondent, the Secretary for the Southern Department, the Duke of Bedford, about 'the several variations in them from those of last session' and one of these was 'a Disposition made for applying the sum of £128,500 . . . to the discharge of so much of the National Debt'. After assuring himself that 'such sums as could be spared, should go to the discharge of the Debt: when I found that the matter would be proposed and push'd in Parliament . . . as there was not Time between the Making up of the Public Accounts, and the bringing the money bills into Parliament, for me to apply for and receive His Majesty's Orders, I determin'd to yield . . . but to do it in such a manner, as that His Majesty might have the whole merit . . . [and] that the claim of the Crown to the disposal of any ballance of the revenue . . . is by no means prejudiced . . . ' The viceroy then particularly requested that this part of the bill should be returned without any alterations or additions. Replying on behalf of the British ministry, Henry Pelham, the First Lord of the Treasury, expressed the royal approval of this use of the surplus, but, at the same time, the king's misgivings that he had not had an opportunity to signify his 'previous consent' to this course of action, as it could, and did, create a dangerous precedent. The reason for the king's 'previous consent' was that the surplus was in the Hereditary Revenue, which was a perpetual grant enjoyed by every monarch since Charles II. From the reign of George I it had been customary for each parliament to grant additional revenue in order to make up the deficiencies of the budget – a surplus was a most unexpected phenomenon.

The publicity given to the activities of Lucas had emphasised his expression of the separatist tradition, previously expounded by Molyneux and Swift, and the question of the disposal of the surplus moneys in the Irish treasury had given these views a potential focus. At that point, insulted by the Irish parliament and the Dublin mob, Lord Harrington was recalled to England. In 1751 he was replaced by the Duke of Dorset, the original patron of Archbishop Stone. Dorset has been described by Horace Walpole as 'a man of dignity, caution and plausibility, and who had formerly ruled Ireland to their universal satisfaction. But he then acted from himself: he was now in the hands of two men most unlike himself, his youngest son, Lord George Sackville, and Dr George Stone, the primate of Ireland. The former a man of very sound parts, of distinguished bravery, and of as honourable eloquence, but hot, hauty, ambitious, obstinate. The primate, a man of fair appearance, of not inferior parts, more insinuating, but by no means less ambitious . . .'.

Undoubtedly the new Lord Lieutenant inherited a difficult and delicate situation. Not entirely unexpectedly, Dorset's second viceroyalty was marked by the outbreak of a violent political quarrel, which operated on several levels and was further complicated by the personalities involved. Unfortunately most of the available evidence is from the side of the Castle and the British ministers; nevertheless, it is possible to discover the outline of the dispute and to hazard some deductions about various aspects of this complicated affair.

The years following the peace of Aix-la-Chapelle were ones of great prosperity 'the present state of Ireland is, in general' declared Lord Orrery in 1752 'as flourishing as possible'. The surplus in the Irish treasury continued and the king, his ministers and the Irish parliament were still in agreement that this money should be applied to the reduction of the national debt. The disagreement arose over the method by which this appropriation should be made: the Irish parliament asserted that they had the sole right to arrange for the disposal of these moneys, while the king and his ministers declared that in view of the nature of the Hereditary Revenue, this money was the king's and therefore his consent was required before it was appropriated. In 1751, when this difficulty again arose, it was at length resolved by having the royal consent written into the preamble of the Act for the appropriation of the money by the British Privy Council, and the Irish parliament reluctantly agreed to the alteration on the bill's return. For most of the eighteenth century the Irish parliament met biennially and the dispute reached its climax when the same situation occurred two years later.

Shortly before the quarrel began the Primate had contrived to offend two very prominent politicians, Thomas Carter, the Master of the Rolls, and Anthony Malone, the Prime Serjeant. Carter, whom Horace Walpole describes as 'an able intriguing man' who had 'constantly fomented every discontent against the lord lieutenants, in order to be bought off', was elderly and had been ill. It was not unusual in the eighteenth century for sons to follow their fathers in office, but this was invariably confined to minor office except in cases of proven ability. Carter, however, wished to secure his son's succession to his great office and Stone refused to support him in this very improper ambition. Carter retaliated by inventing a method of lampooning political opponents in after-dinner toasts to which the opposition press gave wide publicity. In his attitude to Carter's pretensions Stone had the tacit agreement of the Speaker, Henry Boyle, for that office was looked to by Boyle's friend, Anthony Malone, in view of Carter's age and infirmities. However, having been thwarted, and possibly smelling the scent of battle, Carter took on a new lease of life and lived for another decade, dying in 1763. Stone then offended Malone, who wished to have his brother appointed Solicitor-General, by declaring that as Primate and Lord Justice he could not be held to promises which he had made while still Bishop of Clogher.

Meanwhile Stone's political ally, Lord Bessborough, was still continuing his policy of family aggrandisment, and he hoped to acquire the office of Speaker of the House of Commons for his younger son, John Ponsonby, as Speaker Boyle, who was seventy years of age in 1752, could not be long expected to continue in the office which he had held since 1733. Stone supported this scheme and various inducements were used to persuade Speaker Boyle to resign. These probably annoyed Boyle and possibly encouraged him to play for better terms, in any case he refused the overtures of the Chief Secretary, Lord

George Sackville. In January 1754 Stone was still pursuing this plan, writing to Newcastle that, 'I see no person so proper. He [John Ponsonby] has no qualities that can make him dangerous, and his alliance in England must be security for his conduct . . . ' Stone's attitude is of particular interest in view of the fact that the other two traditional Lords Justices, the Primate and the Chancellor were both Englishmen, for since 1725 the views of the Anglo-Irish had been represented by the Speaker alone. This plan was first rumoured prior to the arrival of the Duke of Dorset and the Speaker had then firmly denied that he had any intention of resigning; nevertheless, in view of the realities of the situation it is not improbable that he too began to manipulate the situation to his advantage. If this is the case he was extremely successful.

Henry Boyle, Speaker of the House of Commons from 1733 to 1756 and subsequently 1st Earl of Shannon, is something of an enigma. When he was elected to the Speakership in 1733 a contemporary declared him to be 'very unfit for that station by reason of his natural modesty . . . He is a country gentleman of great good nature and probity, well-beloved, but not of extraordinary abilities . . . ' Stone, although alleging that when he first became Primate, in view of the Speaker's 'age and dignity', he did all that he could to win his support, also discounted him, as did Lord George Sackville, who declared to Henry Pelham that 'he is by no means the leader of the party that makes use of his name'. Certainly Boyle was reluctant to indicate his views to the Castle. When he was summoned by the viceroy to hear the views of the British Privy Council on the Heads of the 1753 Bill of Supply he, and his friends, listened to what the Lord Lieutenant had to say and then arose and departed in silence. Again when presented with a copy of Lord Kildare's memorial to the king expressing 'the discontent with the Lord Lieutenant, the conduct of those in his confidence and the idle stories that were artfully propagated . . . ', Stone informed Newcastle that the Speaker 'thanked my lord Chancellor for sending him Lord Kildare's paper and my Lord Holderness's letter (indicating H.M.'s disapproval of the memorial), without saying a word . . . ' At the same time Boyle was very sociable, his letters to his supporters are skilful and diplomatic, the opposition party centred round him, and he achieved everything that he could legitimately desire; is it possible that he encouraged his contemporaries to underestimate him?

Another political figure who kept extremely quiet, although for different reasons, was the Lord Chancellor, Robert Jocelyn, Lord Newport; 'the Chancellor has always before his eyes,' commented Stone to Newcastle in 1754, 'change of times, fluctuation of power, and retaliation'. A similar reticence was not, however, shown by James, 20th Earl of Kildare, who decided that he should use his great family position to forward the views of the opposition in a document about which Horace Walpole declared 'nothing could be worse drawn: he was too weak to compose a better, and too obstinate to submit to any correction'. Walpole was not noted for his charity, but there was a certain element of truth in his verdict; Lord Kildare's views were important because of his influence rather than his perspicacity. His brother-in-law Henry Fox described him to the Marquis of Hartington as 'a man of strict honour', while on another occasion he wrote: 'he is coming here. I will use all my interest with him . . . if he cannot distinguish between popularity and honour . . . I am sorry for him . . . I again repeat I will be answerable for his sincerity.' The interplay of character and the personal ambitions of these varied personalities undoubtedly contributed to heighten the tensions inherent in the situation, but these intangible elements are very difficult for the historian to assess accurately.

In an attempt to exculpate himself, the Primate wrote to

the Duke of Newcastle in 1754, stating that 'the ill Humours had been long gathering and by time and circumstance were brought to such a head that no Temper nor Management whatsoever could keep them from bursting out'. He declared that Lord Chesterfield had detected signs of it in an incident during his tenure of office, and that only Lord Harrington's insecurity about his position in England had obliged him to treat with the Irish politicians in order to secure at least a nominal tranquillity for his viceroyalty. Stone was probably basically correct in this analysis, as the career of Lucas and the development of the opposition press during the 1740s would sustain this opinion, while the combination of famine, war and the Jacobite rebellion during the decade would temporarily tend to suppress the political discontents which then broke out with added force during the early 1750s. Another element was that one generation of politicians were departing from the scene and their successors were uncertain.

The ground on which battle was finally joined was the rights and privileges of the Irish parliament, a practical interpretation of the theme of Molyneux, Swift and Lucas. 'I do not think they are mad enough to entertain thoughts of separating from England,' wrote Stone of his opponents, 'so that when they declare their abhorrence of setting up an independent interest, they may, in that acceptation of the word be believed. But if they deny that their interest in Parliament and in the country is called the Irish interest, in contra distinction to English, that they say there is a necessity of keeping up such an interest in opposition to English governors, who are always their enemies; if they deny this they disclaim what is their constant language.' Regarding the situation an English politician shrewdly commented that it will hasten the 'progression to a thorough coalescent union between both countries . . . that will be done . . . or indeed will one day do itself.' However, the immediate quarrel continued.

In 1753 there was another surplus and the House of

Commons appointed a committee to draft the Heads of a Bill for its appropriation to the reduction of the national debt. The members of the committee were the Master of the Rolls, Thomas Carter; the Attorney-General, Warden Flood; the Prime Serjeant, Anthony Malone; the Solicitor-General, Philip Tisdall; one of the Commissioners of the Revenue, John Bourke; and John Gore, Counsel to the Revenue Commissioners. Anthony Malone was probably the most outstanding man of his generation, dignified, eloquent and noted for his clear head and sound judgement. In 1752 Stone declared to Newcastle that 'he was born and bred in a popish family . . . his own conversion (it being necessary to his appearing in his profession of the law) does not give such full satisfaction to zealous Protestants', and Stone continues by referring to Malone's 'constant leaning to an Irish interest'. In fact Malone was among the early supporters of measures for Catholic relief.

Anthony Malone dominated the committee which decided to omit the clause acknowledging the king's previous consent to the appropriation of the supply. When the Bill was sent over to England the British Privy Council, advised by its Lord President, Earl Granville, the former Lord Carteret, not only inserted the missing clause but sent a strong letter to the Irish Privy Council on the subject of its omission. The altered bill then came before the House of Commons and it was rejected by five votes, 122 to 117. The viceroy adjourned, and then prorogued, parliament. The royal consent to the appropriation was finally given by sign manual to the Irish treasury. This was the vortex of the problem, but other elements were attracted into the maelstrom, even the adoption of the Gregorian calendar, in 1752, for Great Britain and her dependencies by Act of the Westminster parliament meant that 'all that had ever been said formerly upon the power of binding Ireland by the legislature of England was revived with the greatest acrimony . . .'

Among the victims of the situation was the Surveyor-

General Arthur Nevill Jones, M.P. for Wexford County and a protégé of the Primate's, who had been responsible for some defective military barracks. The House of Commons at first censured Jones, and then, despite his efforts to remedy the defects at his own expense, he was expelled from the House by a majority of 3 votes in November 1753 – although many of those who voted against him considered him to be a man of worth and integrity. The attack on Nevill Jones was a thinly veiled trial of strength between the Castle and the country or Speaker's party, and it produced the unusually large attendance of 239. Criticised for embarking on it, Stone nevertheless considered that, despite the set-back to the government, it rallied 'the credit and property of independent gentlemen' who, ever cautious '. . . resent the behaviour of the King's servants'; he then advocated 'some new model' government otherwise 'it will be vain to attempt the support of English government longer, and he whom his majesty shall appoint to appear formost in that cause will have no other preference than that of being the first sacrifice'.

Following the rejection of the Money Bill, Stone pressed for, and obtained, the dismissal of the major office-holders who had defied the government. At the same time he attempted to detach the Speaker, who resisted all blandishments, realising, as Lord George Sackville wrote to Mr Pelham, that 'the House of Commons is so nearly divided, any one of those who have the least following would, by separating from the rest, give us a clear majority, so that the chiefs of the Opposition for common safety have been obliged to flatter and support the passions and absurd propositions of each other'. The British administration counselled caution and Newcastle wrote to Dorset: 'to take care that there may be persons of credit and ability to carry on the King's business, and such as may be able to do it in the House of Commons . . . The late Chief Justice Singleton (tho' in every respect a most able and deserving man) is thought to be rather worn out in business, and it is late for him to begin to conduct affairs in the House of Commons. My Lord Chief Baron Bowes is certainly an able and very honest man; but neither the one nor the other are in parliament . . . ' Henry Singleton was appointed Master of the Rolls on 11 April 1754. By the following September, Primate Stone was writing to Lord George Sackville that 'the Master of the Rolls grows worse every day . . . He is a melancholy object, and I think can hold out but a very short time.'

The Castle was confronted by a considerable dilemma over the dismissals by the need to find 'persons of credit and ability to carry on the King's business . . . in the House of Commons, for', Newcastle warned Dorset, 'I cannot conceal it from your Grace that his majesty would be extremely concerned to be obliged almost on any account to dissolve this parliament'. Certainly the last precedent for such a dissolution, that of 1713, was hardly encouraging. The Duke of Newcastle was conservative and timid; he was not the man to advocate or approve the widespread changes which the Primate so continually urged.

Among those whose conduct aroused the Primate's displeasure was Nathaniel Clements, the Teller of the Exchequer. Luke Gardiner, the able Deputy-Vice-Treasurer, who had done his best to mediate between the parties was now old and ill, and, complained Stone, 'every day produces some influence of Mr Clements' activity and efficacy. He has the sole direction of the treasury . . . Mr Gardiner has suffered it to drop into his hands . . . His power by it is very distressing to government, and he may be ever depended upon for distressing every administration of which Mr Malone is not the principal . . . The filling his place would be attended with no difficulty . . . Abilities are not requisite; though men of abilities might be found, if they were wanted . . . '! Nevertheless, Stone did advance the theory that 'the whole stock of the nation . . . is now in the hands of one person: and where or how vested is known to him only. The sudden death of that person would at any time occasion great confusion . . . ' Clements and Malone were both connected with the powerful Gore family, nine members of which were sitting in this parliament, and some idea of the ramifications of Clements' power is illustrated by the fact that Mitchel, a banker with whom Clements had deposited large sums of money, had lent Lord Kildare £30,000 and Speaker Boyle was also indebted to Clements. Clements, himself, was cautious and would on a material issue vote with the government, although his friends all voted with the opposition. He also had access to the king through Lady Yarmouth, the royal mistress. The British ministers, despite powerful pressure from both Bessborough and Stone, were very reluctant to dismiss Clements and matters stood thus when the Duke of Dorset was recalled and the Marquis of Hartington, heir to the Duke of Devonshire, sent over in his place. By the time Hartington arrived the Seven Years War was already imminent.

One of the features of Hartington's viceroyalty was the close link between the new viceroy and his father, the former Lord Lieutenant Devonshire. During the critical early months of his viceroyalty Hartington could rely absolutely on his father's powerful influence being exerted to the full over the ministers in London. In addition Hartington possessed Irish connections which extended to all the major conflicting parties: his sisters were married to two sons of Lord Bessborough; his late wife, Lady Charlotte Boyle, had been the heiress of the Cork and Burlington family, the senior branch of the Speaker's family; while politically Hartington was on friendly terms with Henry Fox, the Earl of Kildare's brother-in-law. Finally he was himself a considerable political figure, heir to a great ducal house in England, and possessor of vast estates in Ireland. A cold, aloof man, he was fully conscious of his rank and consequence.

On the appointment of Hartington, the Primate and Lord Bessborough, who with the Chancellor had been appointed Lords Justices on the departure of Dorset, wrote to press their views regarding Clements with the viceroy's father, the 3rd Duke of Devonshire, and they received a very formal and chilly reply. However, Devonshire wrote a private letter to Bessborough, basing it on their personal friendship and family connections, but, pointing out that: 'I cannot conceive it is possible for the Primate to be so ignorant of the King's Ministers and I might . . . say of his nearest relation as to think that what is proposed in that letter likely to be approved . . . when the king thought proper that the D. of Dorset should change employments with my son, I imagine the expediency of that measure might be expected from the consideration that animosity existing or thought to exist in Ireland might be easier composed by a Lieutenant who was not in the country when they took rise. This consideration grew more serious as the probability of a rupture with France increased. I believe it was thought advisable to try if it was possible to quiet matters in Ireland and at the same time to assert the King's just prerogative & government . . . '

Hartington adhered rigidly to this line and distinguished sharply between his public and private relationship with the Ponsonbys, as a month before his arrival he wrote to his brother-in-law: 'whatever my own inclinations may be I am firmly resolved to do nothing but what appears to me to be most for the King's service . . . and as to your private quarrels and animosities give me leave to tell you that I am determin'd to have nothing to do with them'; nevertheless, Hartington was a widower and required a hostess so he concluded his letter: 'I beg my love to my sister . . . pray tell her I expect she will do the honours of the Castle well'.

Shortly after his arrival he had a number of meetings with the leaders of the opposition in consequence of which he wrote to his father: 'by what I can judge they were weary of their opposition and desirous of coming back again, but at the same time were endeavouring to make the best terms they cou'd. However when they saw that I was firm and wou'd not yield they presently acquiesced and . . . once I had assured them that if they behav'd well and supported Government properly, that they shou'd have their share of favour and that the sole management of this country shou'd no longer be in the Primate's hands. They seem'd very well satisfyed and the Speaker came to the following terms with me: that they wou'd concur with me in doing the King's business, that they wou'd not bring on the previous consent &c., that there shou'd be no censures or retrospect . . . Upon the whole by what I can judge myself and by what I hear from others they are all very well pleased and I hope that the Primate and Lord Bessborough are so too . . . indeed they have no reason to complain for I have never given them up to anybody'. 'As to the Primate,' wrote Hartington to Newcastle in May 1755, 'I hope we are very well satisfied with each other, I told him that I wou'd shew him that respect and regard that was due to him and that share of Public favour that was consistent with the present situation of Affairs and that in Private he might depend upon my Friendship; His Grace assur'd me that he was thoroughly satisfy'd and wou'd rest content with whatever share I pleas'd to allot him.'

In order to consolidate this position Hartington, who became Devonshire on the death of his father in December 1755, was obliged to remain in Ireland for a year from May 1755 to May 1756. His residence obviated the need for appointing Lords Justices and consequently the exclusion or inclusion of the Primate in the commission. During this period Hartington used his influence to persuade the Primate to request his own exclusion, at least temporarily, from the commission. Speaker Boyle retired from the Chair, created Earl of Shannon with a pension of £2,000 for thirty-one years; in his place John Ponsonby was elected Speaker but he was not immediately appointed to the commission of Lords Justices, although ultimately he acquired this position also. 'As to the Chancellor,' wrote Hartington to Newcastle, 'I am much pleased with him, he seems to be a very honest plain man, has entered very little into the disputes, and wishes to see an end put to them . . . ' Lord Chancellor Newport duly sailed his little boat into the safe haven of royal approval and was created Viscount Jocelyn. The Earls of Kildare and Bessborough were also gratified as when the Lord Lieutenant returned to England their names with that of the Chancellor were on the commission of Lords Justices.

Having satisfied the major participants, the influential but slightly less prominent politicians also received the viceregal attention. Sir Arthur Gore was promised a peerage, and two years later he was created Earl of Arran. Luke Gardiner died in 1755. Nathaniel Clements succeeded him as Deputy-Vice-Treasurer, making way for Devonshire's relation, Sir Henry Cavendish, who became Teller of the Exchequer and by his inefficiency gave the lie to the Primate's view that 'abilities are not requisite'. Malone, after a respectable interval, succeeded to Speaker Boyle's position as Chancellor of the Exchequer. Fortunately for the government, some of the halt and infirm whom Stone had summoned to his assistance in filling the offices of those dismissed had died, and it was possible to restore all concerned either to their original offices or an equivalent by compensating those who made way for them. However, a disgruntled Carter had to be content with the office of Secretary of State and an additional salary of £1,000 *per annum* instead of his old office of Master of the Rolls.

The Duke of Devonshire returned to England to form an administration in the complicated political situation provoked by the death of Henry Pelham and the outbreak of the Seven Years War. He was succeeded by the Duke of

Bedford. Lord Chancellor Jocelyn died in 1756 and Lord Bessborough in 1758. In March 1758 the Duke of Bedford reluctantly made out the commission of Lords Justices for the Primate, Henry Boyle, Earl of Shannon, and the Speaker, John Ponsonby, and subsequent commissions were similarly inscribed until the death of Stone and Shannon within days of each other in December 1764. Kildare, 'who', as Horace Walpole declared, 'had no talents for governing, and . . . would not unite with anybody that had', was mollified by a marquisate in 1761 and a dukedom in 1766. An uncertain political peace was restored and the war, the age and character of George II, and the temperament of Newcastle guaranteed that there would be no immediate change. Nevertheless the violence of the crisis had once again forced the British ministers to consider the methods by which their power was exercised in Ireland. In July 1755 Lord Lieutenant Hartington wrote to his father that two of the principal legal figures, Lord Chancellor Jocelyn and his subsequent successor, Lord Chief Baron Bowes, had stated to him, 'that this country is growing too big to be governed by any that belong to them and that whether this measure takes place in the present crisis or not it will be a necessary one before . . . long'. An amusing, and not insignificant, sidelight on Devonshire's triumph was supplied by the Duke of Newcastle, who, ever mindful of the exigencies of British politics, by November 1755 was hopefully writing, 'as you are all in good humour I should hope a pension or two would not be objected to and it would ease us here extremely'!

The uncertainty of Devonshire's settlement was revealed, when soon after the arrival of his successor, the Duke of Bedford, the newly-appointed viceroy was confronted by a series of resolutions from the House of Commons on pensions, absentees and other traditional grievances. These resolutions were so worded that Bedford felt they contained an attack on the royal prerogative and, therefore, he refused to transmit them to England. Parliament retaliated by postponing any consideration of the Revenue Bill. Thoroughly alarmed, the British ministry counselled caution and Pitt, who as Secretary of State for the Southern Department was the minister responsible for Ireland as well as for the conduct of the war, advised the viceroy to employ 'all the softening and healing arts of government'. The Irish politicians had found opposition profitable, and were further encouraged in it by the political uncertainties caused by the age of the king, and the well-known antipathy which traditionally existed between the Hanoverians and their heirs. Bedford and his convivial Chief Secretary, Richard Rigby, tried and failed to unite the Kildare and Ponsonby groups. Thus they were forced to fall back on Stone, Shannon and Ponsonby, who had now agreed to work together. In consequence Bedford's second session was easier than his first, and only marred by a riot of the Dublin mob, who suspected that the British administration was contemplating a Union, and a raid on the shores of Belfast Lough by the French commander Thurot.

Thurot's raid in 1760 illustrates both the strategic problem Ireland presented to England and the unprepared state of the country to repel invaders. This continuing situation was partly a consequence of the government's reluctance to embark on any policy that might result in Catholics acquiring arms, and partly, as revealed in the case of Nevill Jones, the result of sheer inefficiency. At the beginning of the Seven Years War there was a widespread belief in England that the French would invade Ireland, and Wesley, who visited Ireland in March 1756, commented that, 'I was surprised to find that all Ireland is in perfect safety. None here has any more apprehension of an invasion, than of being swallowed up in the sea ; every one being absolutely assured, that the French dare not attempt any such thing'; however, about a week later they were a little less sure and Wesley himself was quite convinced of the enemy 'being determined to land in Ireland . . . if God gives them leave'. These fears were borne out when in 1760 the French commander Thurot captured Carrickfergus which he found 'totally unguarded and unprovided . . . the walls were ruinous and in many places incomplete'.

There was a small force inside the town under the command of a Colonel Jennings, whom Walpole described as 'a man formed for a hero; for he had great bravery and a small portion of sense. Thurot, who wanted provisions even more than glory, was content to make a demand of about twenty articles for which he promised to pay. In case of refusal he threatened to burn the place, and then to march to Belfast, a far more opulent and commercial town . . . Some disagreement, however, arising . . . The gates were shut against the invaders – still to the honour of Jennings, for the gates had neither bars nor locks. The fighting began with firing at each other through the gates: but the Irish ammunition soon failing . . . they defended themselves with brickbats, which the rotten condition of the walls easily supplied. When even those stores were exhausted, Jennings retired to the castle . . . The citadel, however, could not hold out without either powder or provisions. It surrendered, and the garrison were made prisoners. Thurot plundered the town, and then sent to demand contributions from Belfast. Ridiculous as this campaign was, it was no joke to the Duke of Bedford . . . The success of Thurot was a glaring comment on the negligence of his grace's administration.' The viceregal forces were mobilised and moved northward to defend Belfast when Thurot, with the Mayor and three of the principal inhabitants of Carrickfergus, put to sea where he was captured by the British navy and died in the engagement. Shortly after Bedford departed determined not to return, and the more astute among the British ministers were more than ever persuaded of the necessity to change the system. At this point on the morning of the 25 October 1760 King George II died at Kensington palace, and the parliament which he had called at his accession, thirty-three years before, was automatically dissolved.

Prior to the summoning of the new parliament, the Irish Privy Council, under the terms of Poynings' Law, was required to certify over to the English Privy Council a number of bills as a reason why parliament should be called. Traditionally one of these bills was always a Money Bill. Considering the state of political opinion the Lords Justices, the Primate, Lord Shannon and Speaker Ponsonby, wrote a long memorandum declaring that such a bill would be certain to be rejected, and would create a ferment at the beginning of the new reign. In this opinion they were supported by the Chancellor of the Exchequer, Anthony Malone, while Lord Kildare declared his support for the bill. The British Privy Council considered that the precedent should be upheld. After considerable altercation the Lords Justices consented to have the bill certified to England and to support it in parliament on its return. A general election was then held in an atmosphere of intense political interest. However, despite the political excitement engendered by the first general election since 1727, when the bill of supply came before the new parliament it passed without difficulty. Kildare received his marquisate and Anthony Malone was dismissed.

The early years of George III's reign were politically tranquil and murmurs about the rapidly increasing pension list and the need to limit the duration of parliament came to nothing. Meanwhile the politicians, who had dominated the reign of George II, were gradually leaving the stage; Carter died in 1763, Primate Stone and Lord Shannon in the closing weeks of 1764 and Lord Chancellor Bowes, who had succeeded Jocelyn in 1757, died in 1767. Kildare became Duke of Leinster in 1766 and he and Anthony

Malone, who enjoyed a great reputation and despite his dismissal from office continued to be consulted by the government on major issues, lived on into the 1770s. Neither the 2nd Earl of Shannon, nor his father-in-law, John Ponsonby, possessed the political skills of their respective fathers, but a new generation was arising when, in 1759, Henry Flood and John Hely-Hutchinson both entered parliament. Flood was the son of Chief Justice Warden Flood; nevertheless, he joined the opposition and quickly gained a brilliant reputation. Hely-Hutchinson, who was a self-made man, joined the government and by 1761 was Prime Serjeant, he was a man of great abilities and possessed of a cynical sense of humour: on one occasion he remarked to the Attorney-General, 'now, Mr Tisdall, that we have done the service of the Government, what do you think if we were to do something for the country', and Tisdall, not to be outdone, replied, 'Mr Hutchinson, ruined! . . . if we attempt that we are undone. The opposition will bear that we should take the emoluments, *but if we lay claim to popularity, we are ruined for ever!*'

No less than six viceroys were appointed during the first seven years of George III's reign, and two of these, Lords Weymouth and Bristol, did not come over to Ireland at all. This rapid succession of Lords Lieutenant partly reflects the fluctuating ministries of the early years of George III, and partly the increasingly unsatisfactory nature of the system. During these years the idea gradually gained ground that the viceroy ought to reside permanently in the country throughout his tenure of office. Various cabinets discussed and endorsed this idea. In 1766, on the appointment of Lord Bristol, the king had tried to persuade Lord Chatham, whose administration recommended the appointment, that he expected Lord Bristol's 'constant residence while he held office'. Nevertheless, Lord Bristol did not set foot in Ireland, and the idea only came to fruition when Lord Townshend, after his arrival in 1767, confirmed that 'the most effectual means to restore vigor to this government would be keeping Ireland under the constant attention of a resident governor'.

The Catholic Committee had been founded in 1760 by Curry, O'Connor and Wyse in an attempt to obtain a degree of social justice by peaceful constitutional means for the loyal, but depressed, majority, and a degree of political recognition for the emerging Catholic middle class. In this they were supported by such statesmen as Anthony Malone. At the same time the early years of George III's reign also saw the emergence of both Catholic and Protestant movements of agrarian discontent, the Whiteboys and the Oakboys. Neither was adverse to that violence and retribution which has poisoned Irish social and political life from generation to generation. The Whiteboy disturbances were largely in Munster and parts of Leinster. In 1766 they resulted in the execution of Father Nicholas Sheehy the parish priest of Clonmel. Sheehy was sympathetic to the Whiteboys, with whom many of his parishioners were affiliated, and he was accused of the murder of a renegade Whiteboy. There is little doubt that his execution was judicial murder engineered by his enemies, and that he was not guilty of the crime of which he was accused. Certainly he was too trusting, and his behaviour in face of the break-down of law and order left something to be desired, but he was probably foolish rather than criminal. His death caused a lasting resentment. He became a popular martyr, and his grave a place of pilgrimage. Thus by the early 1760s the Catholic resurgence was beginning to gain momentum and its leadership was passing from the passive remnant of the Catholic aristocracy, represented by Lords Trimblestown, Kenmare, Fingall and Gormanston, to the more active, but still conservative, middle class, while the agrarian discontent of the masses was beginning to be expressed in acts of sporadic terrorism.

6 The Age of Flood and Grattan, c. 1767–90

GEORGE, 4th Viscount and subsequently 1st Marquis Townshend was forty-three years of age at the time of his appointment to the viceroyalty of Ireland. His previous experience had been almost entirely military. He had an abrasive as well as a convivial personality, which made enemies as well as friends. He was, nevertheless, an administrator of very considerable ability and the stamp of his viceroyalty marked succeeding administrations for the remainder of the century. Townshend's principal achievement was the transfer of parliamentary management from the Irish politicians to the Castle which became, henceforth, the actual centre of executive government and the fountain of all honours and patronage. He was also interested in expanding Irish trade, particularly with the West Indies where Ireland's linens and provisions in exchange for West Indian sugar offered a natural exchange of goods, although contrary to the entrepôt mercantilist policies of Great Britain, and in this area Townshend's success was limited both by Britain's adherence to the Navigation Acts and by the recession of the early 1770s.

Government by a resident viceroy, the nominee and the responsible agent of the king and cabinet in London, demonstrated the separation of the legislature and the executive in Ireland. At the same time the interests of efficient administration automatically emphasised the necessity of bridging the gap between them. This was done through the creation of a solid government or 'Castle' group in the Irish House of Commons, pledged to carry out the policy of the king and his ministers in Great Britain, and rewarded through that government's intermediary, the Lord Lieutenant of Ireland. This party, managed and led by the Chief Secretary, now provided the essential political cohesion between the executive and the legislature in Ireland. It rested partly on the Irish treasury group or 'civil service' M.P.s, partly on members desiring legal or military advancement, partly on social climbers and peerage hunters, and largely on indirect bribery, generally in the form of sinecures, pensions or local patronage. Lord Townshend's work was consolidated by Earl Harcourt, his immediate successor, and during the ten years of their successive administrations, the executive policy pursued by the Castle in the years before the union was laid down.

From the moment an able Lord Lieutenant took up permanent residence a clash with the 'undertakers' was inevitable, and during Lord Townshend's viceroyalty this break was precipitated by two closely related circumstances. From the time of the Seven Years War onwards the British ministers became increasingly concerned with the defence and maintenance of the great empire which they had acquired. Before Lord Townshend left England he had received explicit instructions from the British cabinet to secure the consent of the Dublin parliament to a plan for augmenting the Irish army to approximately 15,000 men. This policy was not only the wish of the ministry but the emphatic, personal command of the king himself. Shortly after Townshend's arrival this plan was laid before the leading Irish politicians who promptly indicated that their support could only be obtained in return for a share of royal patronage 'proportioned to the number of their friends and their weight in the country' and certain personal favours to themselves. Townshend refused. Immediately Ponsonby and his friends turned all their political resources against the Castle, although much of the power and prestige which they were exerting originated in their control of government patronage, and the augmentation bill was rejected. The Lord Lieutenant had two alternatives, either to pay the price they demanded and let the situation continue as before, or to build up a new political party which would look directly to the Castle as the source of all political favour and advancement, receiving its parliamentary lead from the reigning Chief Secretary.

Aware of the British ministry's desire for the augmentation and relying on their exasperation with the continual blackmail of the Irish politicians, Townshend decided on the latter course. The country was at peace, the conservative and aged king was dead. The timid, vacillating and placatory Duke of Newcastle died in 1768, having left the political arena some years before. The tide of the times encouraged the change, and the nervous irresolution of Ponsonby and Shannon completed their downfall. Another circumstance, which strengthened the viceroy, was the passing during the same parliamentary session, 1767–8, of the Octennial Act, limiting the life-span of the Irish parliament to eight years. This ostensibly popular and patriotic measure was originally intended by the British administration as an inducement to persuade the Irish parliament to agree to the unpopular augmentation. However, the octennial elections introduced by this Act automatically struck at the control over the Irish representative system exercised by the great borough owners, for although in the majority of the corporations their control was so absolute that they remained impervious to any increase in the number of elections, nevertheless, the authority of the Irish politicians henceforth received a greater challenge in the counties and in the more open urban constituencies. At the same time a greater opportunity was offered for a different type of member to enter parliament, namely, men who for professional or personal reasons found it convenient to sit in parliament for a relatively short and limited period, and it was frequently to the advantage of these men to support the Lord Lieutenant of the day. To such men the Octennial Act had a particular importance, for before the passing of the Place Act in 1793 Irish M.P.s could not resign their seats during the lifetime of the parliament for which they had been elected. The Octennial Act was followed by the dissolution of parliament and a general election.

When the new parliament met they were assured by the viceroy of the king's personal promise that 12,000 troops would be kept permanently in Ireland except in times of extreme emergency. This reassured the country gentlemen and the new parliament passed the augmentation bill. However, the traditional Money Bill had been certified over to England as a reason for calling the new parliament. This time, when it came before parliament, it was rejected and, as in 1692, this rejection was accompanied by a resolution assigning its reason, namely, because it did not take its rise in the House of Commons. Once again it was the attack on Poynings' Law implicit in the resolution and not the actual rejection which gave offence to the Lord Lieutenant and the British administration. Similarly parliament was not adverse to voting generous supplies. The 'Heads' of a new Money Bill were immediately introduced into the House of Commons where the bill passed easily on its return from England. Nevertheless, the British ministers felt that they could not ignore the implications of the resolution, and, when the Money Bill was passed, the Lord Lieutenant was ordered to follow the example of Lord Sydney in 1692 and to prorogue parliament which had then sat for only three of its usual session of eight months.

During the following fourteen months Townshend embarked on a systematic and expensive plan aimed at establishing a stable government party under the direct control and immediate guidance of the Castle. Ponsonby was dismissed from the Revenue Board and its patronage returned to the Castle, Shannon was deprived of the Mastership of the Ordnance and, at his own request, the Duke of Leinster was struck out of the Privy Council. Hely-Hutchinson, who had gone over to the Castle, received an addition of £1,000 to his sinecure office of Alnager, while Lords Ely, Tyrone and Drogheda, who between them had considerable parliamentary strength, all agreed to support the viceroy. All government patronage was now restored to the Lord Lieutenant, and consequently the great borough owners were thrown upon their natural resources.

Nevertheless, the power of the great magnates was based on their personal control of the Irish representative system and it continued to be such that no government could afford to ignore them completely. In addition to their personal influence they had the 'native' support, as, for instance, reflected in the Dublin mob, which they gained from being an 'Irish' as opposed to an 'English' party. They were an integral part of the Irish ascendancy, whereas the Castle party looked outside Ireland to the British government for guidance and support. Thus an alliance between the administration and one or two of the great political families remained essential for the remainder of the century, especially in times of crisis when normal parliamentary alliances were frequently endangered. Therefore the system inaugurated by Townshend resulted in the Lord Lieutenant becoming the permanent and dominant 'undertaker' but seldom the only one, as his administration still depended on the alliances which he could conclude with the leading Irish politicians, whose power over the government was henceforth restricted rather than abolished.

Parliament reassembled in 1771 and the viceroy's victory was complete when the customary address of thanks to the king for continuing the Lord Lieutenant in office was carried by 132 to 107 votes. It devolved on Ponsonby as Speaker to present it; he refused and resigned his office. The two subsequent Speakers of the Irish House of Commons, Edmund Sexton Pery and John Foster, were definitely the servants of the House and although often consulted by government did not combine administrative office with the Speakership, a fact which was clearly recognised when John Foster resigned the office of Chancellor of the Exchequer on his election to the Speakership in 1785. In September 1772 Townshend was recalled; he had resided in the country for almost five years and he, himself, swore in Lord Harcourt thus obviating the need for appointing Lords Justices, who, during the remainder of the century were only appointed on three occasions, namely, when the Duke of Rutland died in office in October 1787, when the Marquis of Buckingham was ill following the regency crisis, and returned to England in 1789, and on the recall of Earl Fitzwilliam in 1795.

These years mark the apex of the power and prestige of the Anglo-Irish ascendancy. Nowhere was their influence and taste more clearly shown than in the city of Dublin. The seventeenth-century plantation towns with their familiar diamond pattern, along with various smaller experiments, had accustomed the Irish gentry to the idea of town planning, and Dublin was to benefit greatly from their enlightened application of this method of urban development. In 1757 the Irish parliament appointed a Commission for making wide and convenient streets. It gave the Commissioners authority to implement their decisions by the compulsory purchase of houses, which obstructed their plans, along with generous parliamentary grants to implement their decisions and the right to raise additional revenue by levying duties on the sale of coal, playing-cards and the use of club premises. Examples of streets planned by the Commission are Lower Sackville

(O'Connell) Street and Westmoreland Street. They also built Carlisle (O'Connell) Bridge. In the years following the Union, their work was complemented by the Commission for paving and lighting, formed in 1806.

A parallel interest in fine buildings resulted in parliamentary support for the erection of some of the most magnificent public buildings in Europe. These included the Parliament House itself, the great façade of Trinity College, the Royal Exchange (now the City Hall), the Customs House, the Four Courts and the King's Inns. The last three were designed by James Gandon, whom John Beresford, M.P. for Waterford and First Commissioner of the Revenue, brought over from England to design the new Customs House which was begun in 1781. The Four Courts had originally been planned by Thomas Cooley, architect of the Royal Exchange, but on Cooley's death in 1784 the project passed to Gandon. The other leading architect at the end of the century was Francis Johnston. Francis Johnston was born in Armagh and the historic General Post Office in what was then Sackville Street and is now O'Connell Street was built to his design between 1815 and 1820. However, the dominant architectural influence on Dublin's great public buildings is indisputably that of James Gandon who lies buried in Drumcondra churchyard, while his memorial lies around him in the beautiful city which he did so much to adorn.

At the end of the seventeenth century private houses in the capital were narrow and gabled. During the eighteenth century in the better residential districts these gradually gave way to the wide streets and squares of plain, parapeted, red-brick Georgian houses which, with their substantial panelled doors, framed with pillars and surmounted by varied lacy fanlights, remain so dominant a feature of Dublin today. Arthur Young in the 1770s found them 'good and convenient. Mr La Touche's in Stephen's Green, I was shown as a model of this sort, and I found it well contrived and finished elegantly . . . ' This interest in urban development although most marked in the capital was not confined to it but spread through the provinces. Armagh was largely rebuilt by Primate Robinson and Edmund Sexton Pery, Speaker of the House of Commons from 1772 to 1785, sponsored extensive developments in his native city of Limerick.

Although Anglo-Irish society comprised a very narrow section of the community, nevertheless, it reflected a surprisingly wide spectrum of social usage and public responsibility. For instance, the contrast was considerable between the intellectual elegance of Lord Charlemont's salons at Charlemont House or Marino, the semi-regal splendour of the Duke of Leinster's establishments at Carton or Leinster House, and the incredible scene of bacchanalian squalor which greeted Sir Jonah Barrington when he paid a surprise morning visit to his brother. 'We are not overmuch given to buy or read books', declared Primate Boulter in 1735 – four years after the foundation of the well-patronised Dublin Society. However, as the century progressed, an interest in intellectual and literary pursuits increased, stimulated by education and sustained by increasing prosperity and leisure. The speculative and theoretical interests which the Dublin Society encouraged were particularly congenial to the cultural climate of the late eighteenth century and they found their expression in the foundation of the Royal Irish Academy in 1785 to promote the study of 'science, polite literature and antiquities'.

The ties of the Anglo-Irish with England were complex. First of all they were based on security, for, as Lord Charlemont observed, 'ill confiding in the paucity of their numbers, [they] had been long accustomed to look up to England for support, and were ever fearful of offending that kingdom, from whose powerful interference, in case of emergency, they hoped for protection'. Secondly, they were based on intermarriage and family connection. The effects of the Ponsonby-Cavendish marriages have already been noticed. Another connection was formed by the marriages of the daughters of the 2nd Duke of Richmond: Emily married James Fitzgerald, 1st Duke of Leinster and premier peer of Ireland; Louisa was married to Thomas Conolly, the richest commoner and most prominent country gentleman in Ireland; while their elder sister Caroline was the wife of Henry Fox, 1st Lord Holland. The third bond was that created by friendship and a similar and sometimes common education, for many of the Irish gentry completed their formal education either at Oxford or Cambridge. Prior to the foundation of the King's Inns in Dublin in 1783, a legal education, popular with the country gentry and aspiring politicians as well as lawyers, could only be obtained at the Inns of Court in London. Thus before the Irish ascendancy there was always the example of the elegance and affluence of the English governing class, whose landed wealth had been consolidated down the centuries and was being increasingly augmented by new commercial fortunes; consequently, many Irishmen acquired aspirations which their resources were ill-equipped to sustain and probably in no field was this dichotomy more marked than in that of architecture. Maria Edgeworth exposes the dilemma in which many of the Irish gentry found themselves by the early 1780s: 'at that time, in Ireland,' she recollects, 'many of the gentry were in remarkable extremes as to their dwelling houses. Some travelled gentlemen erected superb mansions disproportionate to their fortunes, and at last were obliged to sell an estate to pay for a house; or at best they lived in debt, danger, and subterfuge the rest of their days, nominally possessors of a palace, but really in dread of a gaol. Others . . . marking these misfortunes, they determined never to build; so lived on in wretched houses out of repair, windows without sashline . . . without . . . the comforts and decencies of life. Others shunned these extremes . . . they struck out a new half mode of going wrong. These would neither build a palace nor live in a hovel; but they planned the palace, built offices to suit, and then turned stable and coach-house into their dwelling house . . . leaving the rest to fate, and to their sons.'

In the 1720s Swift in his *Short view of the State of Ireland,* commented that the seats of the nobility and gentry were 'all in ruins' and that no new ones were being built. This was not strictly true, as Castletown, Speaker Conolly's great mansion in Co. Kildare, was already under construction. Designed by the Italian architect, Alexandro Gallilei, and completed under the direction of Edward Lovett Pearce, architect of the new Parliament House, Castletown was the oldest and certainly the most magnificent of the Irish palladian houses. Shortly afterwards the Earl of Kildare decided to rebuild Carton and this project was completed by the German architect Richard Cassels, who also designed Leinster House in Kildare Street, Dublin, for Lord Kildare's son, the 1st Duke of Leinster. Cassels was the leading architect of the mid-eighteenth century, and his public buildings included the Lying-in Hospital, begun in 1751.

Irish Georgian houses have long been famous for the exquisite plaster-work which was widely used in their interior decoration. Like the Irish glass and silver of this period its inspiration was originally foreign but, nevertheless, Irish craftsmen soon became extremely skilled creating a graceful beauty uniquely their own. For instance although the work of Paul and Philip Francini can be seen in the splendid ceiling of the salon at Carton, representing the courtship of the gods, the birds on the staircase of St Saviour's Orphanage are the work of Robert West, who also designed the house. Towards the end of the century the rococo plaster-work was superseded by the more formal designs made popular by the Adam brothers,

141

whose principal follower in Ireland was Michael Stapleton. These neo-classical designs made a considerable use of moulds which led to the decline of the free-style craftsman. The English manufacturer and entrepreneur, Thomas Wedgwood, established an agency in Dublin through which he conducted a brisk trade in medallions and chimney-pieces as well as vases and dinner-services. One room in Dublin Castle is beautifully decorated with Wedgwood medallions.

At the beginning of the century the formal Dutch style of house and garden, like Mount Ievers Court in County Galway, was popular. Following the completion of Castletown enthusiasm for palladian houses became widespread and landscape gardening fashionable with an increasing interest in rare botanical plants. In 1776 Chief Baron Foster, the father of Speaker Foster, had in his garden at Collon in Couty Louth approximately 1,700 European and American plants, while at the end of the century the Bellevue conservatories of Peter La Touche, M.P. for Co. Leitrim, were famous for the beauty and variety of their foreign plants. Palladian architecture was eventually superseded by Gothic and Ireland has one remarkable example of the transition, Castle Ward in County Down. Built in the 1760s Castle Ward stands as a perpetual monument to the divergent tastes of the builder, Bernard Ward, M.P. for County Down and 1st Lord Bangor, and his wife, Lady Anne, who built it with two fronts one classical and the other Gothic, a lack of agreement which was further reflected in a similar division in the interior decoration of the rooms. Lord Bangor was careful to emphasise his view by having his portrait painted with his classical design in his hand! Domestic tranquillity was not a noted feature of this schizophrenic establishment.

Other aspects of Irish society displayed a similar duality of thought and behaviour. For instance, at Colganstown, County Dublin, the diners could not resist the sport of shooting the heads off the plaster-work birds which ornamented the dining-room. In the 1730s Lord Orrery commented that 'a right jolly "glorious memory" Hibernian never rolls into bed without having taken a sober gallon of claret to his own share. You wonder perhaps what this animal is? It is a Yahoo that toasts the glorious and immortal memory of King William in a bumper without any other joy in the Revolution than that it has given him a pretence to drink so many more daily quarts of wine . . . ' The traditional toast on these occasions was 'the glorious, pious, and immortal memory of the good and great King William, who delivered us from Popery, slavery, arbitrary power, brass money, and wooden shoes': Sir Jonah Barrington commented, 'could his Majesty King William learn in the other world that he has been the cause of more broken heads and drunken men since his departure than all his predecessors, he must be the proudest ghost, and most conceited skeleton that ever entered the gardens of Elysium' – a curious epitaph on that austere Calvinist monarch! In the 1740s Chesterfield, commenting on the consequences of the 5,000 tuns of wine imported annually, wished that God would 'turn all the wines in Ireland sour'.

Excessive drinking and duelling were common features of Irish society. Political duels were notorious: 'amongst other qualifications for public station,' wrote Lord Townshend to John Hely-Hutchinson, 'the gladiatorial is one of the most essential in your country'; the *Belfast Newsletter* reported that 22 duels were fought during the course of the 1783 election for County Cork. Stories about the wilder and more irresponsible sections of the Irish gentry are endless, varying from the harmlessly eccentric to the criminal and the psychopathic. Many of these characteristics were personified by Beauchamp Bagenal, M.P. for Co. Carlow and an enthusiastic leader of the Volunteer movement in that county. He usually sat down to dinner with a brace of pistols, one of which he used to tap his cask of claret and the other to encourage his guests to drink it. During his adventurous career he had on one occasion abducted a Spanish duchess and, on another, broken into an Italian convent – in search of a nun. The wilder actions of the more irresponsible gentry and squireens included the abduction of heiresses. The penurious and unscrupulous even formed clubs for this purpose, the attraction of which lay in the fact that a married woman's property belonged to her husband. This practice only declined after two abductors were executed following the Kilkenny Assizes in 1780.

The viceroy who succeeded Lord Townshend in 1772, and consolidated his policies, was a man of a very different type. Lord Harcourt was an orthodox whig of the old school, he had been governor to the king following the death of Frederick, Prince of Wales, and prior to his arrival in Ireland he had been ambassador in Paris. Lord Townshend's policies proved expensive, and combined with the trade recession of the early 1770s to produce an increasing deficit in the revenue. Harcourt endeavoured unsuccessfully to retrench, one of his measures being to reunite the Revenue Board, which Townshend had divided into the Boards of Customs and Excise in order to acquire more consequential positions. Confronted by this financial stringency the House of Commons became exercised once more over one of their traditional grievances, the absentee proprietors, who drew their incomes from the country while contributing nothing to its welfare. Likewise concerned about the deficit in the revenue, the Castle underestimated the strength of the absentees' influence in British politics and introduced a tax on absentee rents. The ensuing clamour nearly deafened Lord North's administration and the Lord Lieutenant was hastily ordered to sink the offending measure.

These instructions stretched to the utmost the diplomacy of Lord Harcourt and his astute Chief Secretary, Sir John

Blaquiere, for the measure which had been for so long a favourite project of the Irish House of Commons, could not be quietly cushioned; it had to be publicly rejected. This was achieved by exploiting the fears and jealousies of the Irish landowners. Irish taxation was largely indirect taxation and it was carefully insinuated that this projected tax on the incomes of absentees might gradually develop into a general land-tax as in England. After the government had carefully prepared the ground, the measure was introduced into the House of Commons and during the debate Chief Secretary Blaquiere, in a very skilful speech, announced that the administration had decided to allow a 'free vote' on this very controversial issue, declaring that 'if Administration should take any part in it it will be to follow and not to lead the wishes of this House'. The Irish landowners panicked at what they construed to be a concealed threat to their interests and, joining with the members under the influence of the absentee landlords, they rejected the measure. The division lists were scarcely closed when the majority of M.P.s realised their mistake. However, by then it was too late, and the government firmly refused to reopen the debate. In his despatch to Lord North the viceroy commented that, 'such an instance of capriciousness and instability is perhaps hardly to be met with . . . and will mark to his Majesty . . . that wild inconsistent conduct which every Lord Lieutenant has to encounter in a much more forcible and comprehensive manner than words can express'.

The outbreak of the American war highlighted the dilemma of the ascendancy. Theoretically the Americans were fighting for those same rights and liberties which they themselves had tried so often to exert, but practically they lacked the strength and the security which would have enabled them to embark on military rather than parliamentary defiance, while emotionally their ties and traditions with England were closer and deeper. The predictable does not always happen in history but on this occasion it did. The speech from the throne at the opening of parliament in October 1775 referred to the rebellion in America. The Irish parliament immediately drew up an address expressing their own loyalty to the Crown and their 'abhorrence' of and 'indignation' at the situation in America. The address had a comfortable majority in a house which was only half-full; nevertheless, it was not unopposed, and Lord Harcourt noted that 'the debate was conducted with great violence on the part of the opposition'. Outside parliament the Americans had many sympathisers, particularly among the Ulster Presbyterians, but the Catholic population remained quiet and loyal. Their behaviour was rewarded in 1778 when Luke Gardiner, grandson of the late Deputy-Vice-Treasurer, successfully introduced the first major measure of Catholic Relief. However, this was not the first of these Bills to come before the Irish House of Commons, as there had been a number of unsuccessful measures proposed in the years between 1762 and 1778 by M.P.s like John Monk Mason and Sir Hercules Langrishe and supported by politicians like Anthony Malone.

The latter part of the eighteenth century was an age of uncommon brilliance in the Irish House of Commons, and three men in particular, Henry Flood (1732–91), Henry Grattan (1746–1820), and John Fitzgibbon (1748–1802), stand out among their peers, who included men like John Foster, Speaker of the House of Commons and John Hely-Hutchinson, Provost of Trinity College in 1774 and also Secretary of State from 1771. Satisfactory biographies of Flood and Fitzgibbon have still to be written, as has an analysis of Grattan's position and achievements for which there is very much more material. Flood and Fitzgibbon were probably both intellectually superior to Grattan, and they tended to rely on the dubious force of logic as a political weapon to a much greater extent than the more imaginative and emotional Grattan. 'Mr Grattan', wrote Barrington, 'did not always foresee the remote operation of his projects. He was little adapted to labour on the detail of measures', and possibly this was both the strength and weakness of his career. Fitzgibbon cared nothing for popularity, Flood was ambivalent towards it, but Grattan liked and courted it. The Duke of Portland, who knew him well in the period following 1782, considered him 'a very well intentioned & honestly disposed person' but 'that he is still [1783] so far infected with the contagious Part of that Passion as still to sacrifice his own opinions at that shrine'. Nevertheless, both Flood and Fitzgibbon lacked Grattan's flexibility and the warmth of personality which endeared him to his generation.

Despite the passing of the Act of Union, Henry Grattan must be accounted among the most fortunate of politicians as he was undoubtedly one of the most attractive personalities of his age. He belonged to an established Dublin family – although at variance with his father, a former Recorder of Dublin and M.P. for Dublin city from 1761 until his death in 1766. Three months before Grattan entered parliament, Flood, who had been the most brilliant and consistent member of the opposition for sixteen years, accepted the office of Vice-Treasurer and joined the King's servants; Grattan stepped into the vacuum and Flood, who remained Vice-Treasurer until 1781 watched Grattan reap what was to a considerable degree the reward of his labours. Thus Grattan entered parliament at precisely the right moment and he achieved his great success while still comparatively young. For the remainder of his life he enjoyed great power without the responsibility, and without the need for compromise which office inevitably brings and which, as in the case of Flood, can so easily tarnish the lustre of the most brilliant reputation. Flood and Fitzgibbon were both wealthy men; neither required the emoluments of office, while the £50,000 which the Irish parliament voted Grattan in gratitude for his services provided the financial equivalent of an official salary without its disadvantages and responsibilities.

The point of not accepting office was elevated to a virtue by both Grattan and his patron, Lord Charlemont, on the grounds that 'office in Ireland was different from office in England; *it was not a situation held for Ireland, but held for an English Government, often in collision with, and frequently hostile to Ireland.*' Nevertheless, Grattan agreed with Charlemont when the latter wrote to Fox in April 1782, '*I am an Irishman* . . . at the same time . . . I most sincerely and heartily concur with you in thinking that *the interest of England and Ireland cannot be distinct* . . . ' Apart from the overlap in these two views, the basic argument has a certain speciousness: it raises the question of how they propose to implement their policies if they insist in always remaining outside all governments. Similarly a refusal to undertake the burdens of office almost certainly results in a failure to realise the practical problems confronting an administration attempting to implement the popular policies, which the opposition enjoy the credit of advocating. Political achievement depends on realising and exploiting the political realities actually existing, rather than imagined or desired, at a given moment in time. The attitude of Charlemont and Grattan encouraged, where their participation might have moderated, this division between ideal policies and practical realities thereby adding to the tensions which built up during the final decade of the century.

It is possible that both Charlemont, who was a poor speaker, and Grattan, who disliked detail and frequently acted on impulse, unconsciously used this argument as an excuse, for it was certainly an unusual attitude for an eighteenth-century politician to adopt however patriotic his views. Grattan, who had probably the best political instinct of any member of the Irish House of Commons during the century, may have realised the limitations of his great gifts, and that he was not a second Chatham born to seal a brilliant oratorial reputation with a splendid ministerial career – despite the limitations of Irish office. Even the Union did not destroy Grattan's political career as his flexibility enabled him to transplant easily and successfully into the imperial parliament, a transition which Flood had failed to achieve some twenty years earlier. Indeed the triumphs of Grattan appear to have been balanced by the misfortunes of Flood, as Grattan's virtues shine in patriotic memory when contrasted with Fitz-gibbon's alleged iniquities. Nevertheless, the arguments employed by both Flood and Fitzgibbon were subse-quently shown to have an equal veracity, yet the tide of the times was with Grattan's instincts rather than Fitzgibbon's logic, and subsequent generations, with the benefit of hindsight, have judged them accordingly. Grattan's great strength – and Fitzgibbon's corresponding weakness – was his realisation of the dictum that 'where there is no vision the people perish'; the successful politician requires imagination as well as logic. Possibly the presence and influence on Irish politics of Grattan and Fitzgibbon con-jointly was to defeat the one man who possessed these qualities and was in a position to use them, the British Prime Minister, William Pitt.

It is very difficult to arrive at an accurate assessment of these three men. Flood and Fitzgibbon appear to have left few personal papers from which their views and problems can be ascertained. On the other hand Grattan's son, dis-playing a filial regard which occasionally grates on the modern reader, published a five-volume biography which not only documents his father's life but gives his opinion of his political opponents. For lack of other evidence this opinion has frequently stuck, so that the reader, often at several removes from the source, accepts Grattan at his own and his son's valuation, while he views Grattan's political opponents through Grattan's eyes. Irish history has tended to regard men as either heroes or villains but seldom as that complicated mixture which makes a human being. Along with this attitude has gone a tendency to view events in a climate of feeling which is often very different from that in which they occurred.

The years from the recall of Earl Harcourt in January 1777 to the recall of Earl Temple in May 1783 cover the period of the American Revolution. The territories Great Britain had won during the Seven Years War, and which had been confirmed at the Peace of Paris in 1763, had humiliated her opponents and incurred their envy. Consequently, when the rebellion of her colonies developed into a prolonged struggle, they reopened the conflict. By 1779 Great Britain was at war with most of Europe, either in an active or passive capacity. This national emergency led to the withdrawal of troops from Ireland, where the army served both for defence and, in the absence of a police force, to maintain civil order.

At the beginning of the war Lord North had suggested the employment of German mercenaries for the defence of Ireland, but Harcourt had pointed out to him that, 'foreigners may, either from their ignorance of the language, or from other causes, not be applicable to many of the civil purposes in which the Irish army is necessarily employed': in 1799 Lord Cornwallis was to make the same point regarding the posting of Russian troops to Ireland, namely, that they would be 'unacquainted with our language and the nature of our Government'. It was to meet this civil and military need that the Volunteer movement arose in 1778. Many of the Irish gentry had served in the army and regiments, uniforms, ranks, parades and reviews were soon the order of the day. At its inception the movement was entirely protestant, though not exclusively Anglican, and it had the sympathy and support of the Catholics. The dilemma which the Volunteers presented to the government was that they were a force outside the control of the administration but at the same time they were a necessity for national defence.

Lord Harcourt had been succeeded by Lord Buckinghamshire early in 1777. The new viceroy was a mild man of moderate abilities inadequately supported by his Chief Secretary, Sir Richard Heron, whose 'talents', as Buckinghamshire himself admitted, 'do not enable him to take the least active part in Parliament. Consequently, upon every unforseen Motion, the House runs wild, and those who should support follow their own caprice . . . and assert that they could not distinguish what was really the wish of Government . . . ' Anxious to conduct an honourable administration with the maximum economy, Buckinghamshire decided to rely upon the support of the country gentlemen, one of whose leaders was his brother-in-law Thomas Conolly. He discovered too late that 'beyond a certain line you can not press for the intended conduct of Independent Gentlemen'.

In the pressures created by the war the Commons re-collected their long-standing political and economic grievances, particularly following the customary embargo which had been placed on the export of Irish provisions at the beginning of hostilities. Although contracts from the armed forces had resulted in a scarcity of provisions and high prices, nevertheless, this was considered a grievance and a leading cause of the country's incipient bankruptcy—rather than the fall in customs duties and the drain of money paid to troops serving abroad. Backed by the armed power of the Volunteers, and broken loose from the authority of the Castle, the Commons demanded and obtained free-trade in 1779–80.

This success was followed by the direction of their new power to remedying their other long-standing grievances. The British government and its representatives Lord Carlisle, the Duke of Portland and Earl Temple were powerless to resist their demands. In 1781 a Habeas Corpus

Bill was passed and the independence of judicial tenure conceded. Then in 1782 Poynings' Law was amended so that the only remaining restriction on Irish legislation was the royal veto. The constitutional concessions were completed by the repeal of the 1719 Declaratory Act, and, at Flood's insistence, by an Act of the British parliament renouncing the right which the 1719 Act declared, namely, to legislate for Ireland and to act as the final court of judicature for Irish law suits. Flood had been dismissed from his Vice-Treasureship in 1781. However, he had failed to regain the leadership of the opposition which had now definitely passed to Grattan and Yelverton, the architects of the 1782 constitution.

Despite this separatist agitation the loyalty of the Irish parliament to the British connection was, perhaps, never more clearly expressed than on 4 December 1781, the day that Yelverton was to introduce his motion for the amendment of Poynings' Law. News had just arrived of Lord Cornwallis' surrender at Yorktown, and, wrote Lord Carlisle, 'Mr Yelverton postponed his intended motion, and, with a propriety which was felt universally by the House, proposed an address to His Majesty full of loyalty to his royal person ... expressive of the firmest attachment to his Majesty and to the interests of Great Britain'; the address was carried by a majority of 167 to 37. Religious reforms accompanied political concessions: the Sacramental Test had been repealed in 1780, and, in 1782, Gardiner successfully introduced a further measure of Catholic Relief.

The disasters of the American war were a profound psychological shock to the politically involved classes in England. They began to query the structure of a government which could preside over such defeats. The result of this introspection was a two-pronged movement for reform: a streamlining of government through the exclusion of sinecures along with a general policy of economy, and a questioning of the nature of the electoral system by which members were returned to parliament. Ireland, which had shared the colonial grievances of the Americans, now became interested in the parliamentary grievances of the British opposition. This interest was particularly strong among the Volunteers, who represented a much wider section of the community than the exclusively Anglican parliament. Ideas for political reform found a ready response in the independent and democratically inclined North, which, being largely protestant if not Anglican, had participated to a greater degree in the Volunteer Movement than the rest of Ireland because, despite the emergency, the fear of arming Catholics had continued. To further these proposals for parliamentary reform in February 1782 the Ulster Volunteers called a Convention at Dungannon in County Tyrone. The delegates assembled and decided to hold another larger meeting in Dublin in November 1783. Among the motions which came before the Dungannon convention was a resolution drawn up by Grattan, without the knowledge or consent of Flood or Charlemont, which stated: 'that we hold the right of private judgment, in matters of religion to be equally sacred in others as in ourselves; that we rejoice in the relaxation of the PENAL LAWS against our ROMAN CATHOLIC FELLOW SUBJECTS, and that we conceive the measure to be fraught with the happiest consequences to the union and prosperity of the inhabitants of Ireland.' This significant motion was proposed by a Mr Pollock and seconded by the Rev. Mr Black, a Presbyterian minister, and it passed with only two dissentient voices.

The general of the Volunteers was the liberal, but cautious, Lord Charlemont, whom Grattan only slowly converted to his pro-Catholic viewpoint. In Dublin Lord Charlemont's leadership was unsuccessfully challenged by Frederick Augustus Hervey, Earl of Bristol and Bishop of Derry. The only common interest of these two peers was that they were both great builders and patrons of the arts. Lord Bristol's views were so extreme that shortly afterwards he nearly got arrested for high treason, despite his great name and profession. The moderate plans of the Convention for parliamentary reform were presented to the Irish House of Commons by Flood, who created an unfavourable impression by appearing in Volunteer uniform, as the majority of the House of Commons had become alarmed by the radical language of the Volunteers. Consequently they were beginning to share the views of the government regarding the existence of so powerful an armed body in time of peace outside the control of parliament or the administration; for instance when the Duke of Portland arrived in 1782 he found 5,000 regular troops under his direction and 100,000 armed men outside his authority. In addition the fears of the Commons were not allayed by the behaviour of the Earl-Bishop, who wished, although prevented by Flood and Charlemont, to introduce into the convention the question of the Catholic franchise supported by Grattan. Under these circumstances the Irish parliament rejected both this and subsequent reform bills.

Insecurity lay at the foundations of Irish politics, and, in the last resort, the fear which had created the Irish representative system of the eighteenth century also hardened and sustained it. Apart from the obvious difficulty of seeing the need for removing 'the beam that is in thine own eye', the attitude of the Irish parliament to reform was complicated, and at least three separate strands of opposition are discernible. Of these self-interest is clearly the most apparent but, perhaps, the least important. Lord Mornington attributed their attitude to 'alarm upon the subject of the Roman Catholics' pretensions to a right of suffrage, and by a total disapprobation of the violence which has appeared in Dublin'. Also there was the question of the degree and the nature of the reform. Agreement to specific reform was difficult, while opposition was both easier and apparently less hazardous. Thus in 1784 the Irish parliament as a whole adopted the latter course, and the Volunteer movement foundered on this divisive rock.

The government was also against it but for very different reasons; 'in England it is a delicate question,' Rutland wrote to Pitt, 'but in this country it is difficult and dangerous in the last degree'. Pitt, with his usual grasp of essentials, was concerned that 'we may keep the Parliament but lose the people', – an ironic comment on the future Act of Union. Lord Mornington summed up the situation when he remarked 'that all English government will become utterly impracticable, from the moment that any alteration is admitted in the representation of the people'. An irresponsible but corruptible parliament, difficult though it might occasionally be, was nevertheless preferable to a reformed one, answerable for its virtue to a wider section of public opinion.

The constitution of 1782 completed the separation of the legislature from the executive, and for the remainder of its life the Irish parliament enjoyed great privilege and little responsibility. Failure to adopt some measure of reform in face of the developing Catholic and Presbyterian middle classes was slowly isolating parliament from a growing section of the informed and propertied community, and the decline of the Volunteer movement was marked by a growing sympathy between educated Catholic and protestant non-conformists. In other respects also Grattan's parliament was at least to some extent an anachronism within the imperial context of the eighteenth century. One consequence of the independence gained by the constitutional changes of 1782–3 was to make the position of the Irish parliament nearly as impossible as that institution could make the situation of the Irish executive. The remaining years of the 1780s saw two illustrations of this problem: the failure of the commercial negotiations in 1785 and the regency crisis in 1789.

The legislative independence of the Irish parliament had been hastily granted during a period of ministerial weakness in England. Given under pressure, its implications had not been fully envisaged, for what was actually granted in 1782 was a form of dominion status rather than home rule. Thus technically Ireland could, with the consent of the king, not only regulate her internal affairs but conduct her own foreign policy and impose her own customs tariffs, even against English goods. This last possibility became a very real temptation during the depression of 1783–4. The combination of the constitutional with the commercial concessions had resulted in Ireland, apart from the East India Company's monopoly, enjoying an equal trade with England's colonies without being bound by the Navigation Acts, which were the cornerstone of Great Britain's mercantilist policy. It was this confused and complicated situation which the commercial negotiations attempted to clarify.

The commercial resolutions were first introduced into the Irish parliament in February 1785. Subsequently considered and amended by the British parliament, they were to be the foundations of a treaty between the British and Irish parliaments which would iron out some of the anomalies in the relationship between the two kingdoms. England was prepared to confirm Ireland in the privileges which she had acquired, and in return England, despite the circumstances in which she lost the American colonies, still hoped for a contribution towards the expenses of maintaining the empire from her remaining dependencies. This imperial contribution, 'to be applied together with other monies voted here [in England] for naval services, and to be accounted for, together with them, to the Parliament of this country. There can be but *one navy* for the empire at large . . . ', was probably the greatest stumbling-block to the success of Pitt's scheme, particularly as he considered that the appropriate source of the contribution was the

Hereditary Revenue. This might have been a logical source, but in view of the conflict of the 1750s, which Fox and North hastened to recollect, it was hardly a tactful suggestion.

Opposition to the scheme in both parliaments was largely directed by the British opposition leaders, Fox and North. During the spring of 1785 Pitt allowed ample time for a full discussion of the issues involved. The fears of the English merchants and manufacturers were heard in detail and included such arguments as: Ireland's geographical position would make her the emporium of imperial trade; the inefficiency of her revenue officers in applying the revenue laws strictly outside the larger ports would ruin the West Indian planters, whose prosperity was already declining; and the cheapness of her labour would destroy the prosperity of the Lancashire manufacturers. Among those who gave evidence on this last point was the father of the nineteenth-century Chief Secretary and Prime Minister, Sir Robert Peel.

Largely to meet these complaints the resolutions were expanded from eleven to twenty, and on their return to the Irish parliament there was a violent and lengthy debate in the House of Commons on the night of the 12–13 August 1785; afterwards Lord Lieutenant Rutland wrote to Pitt that, 'the speech of Mr Grattan was, I understand, a display of the most beautiful eloquence perhaps ever heard, but it was seditious and inflammatory to a degree hardly credible . . . ' The result was a government majority, 127 to 108, which was too small to allow a bill to be brought in with any hope of success and the project lapsed. 'The current was against it', wrote Rutland, 'and it would have been in vain in the existing state of things here, to contend with it.' 'I had hoped', Pitt replied, 'that neither prejudice nor party could on such an occasion have made so many proselytes against the true interests of the country . . . we must wait for times and seasons for carrying it into effect

. . . ' A good harvest in 1785 relieved the immediate distress of the preceding years, while the bounties assigned by Foster's corn law of 1784 had given fresh impetus to Irish agriculture. When Rutland's viceroyalty was abruptly terminated by his untimely death in 1787, the Irish administration appeared both prosperous and successful.

Nevertheless, the unsolved problem of the relationship between the two countries remained in the minds of the English ministers, successive Irish administrations, and even in the Irish parliament itself, for only the moderation of the members of the Irish opposition, who were usually loud in claiming their powers but cautious in using them, allowed the anomalous situation to continue for so many years. Rutland expressed his doubts when he remarked to Pitt, 'were I to indulge a distant speculation, I should say that without *an union* Ireland will not be connected with Great Britain in twenty years longer'. Events were to prove him right, although the most important period of his viceroyalty was devoted to formulating a system which, had it been successful, might have avoided this eventuality. Agrarian disturbances had continued and in 1787, under the influence of Fitzgibbon, an Act, known as the Whiteboy Act, was passed introducing into Ireland both the provisions of the famous British Riot Act of 1716 and in addition stringent measures against all who administered or voluntarily entered into illegal oaths.

The Marquis of Buckingham, an able but difficult man, succeeded the Duke of Rutland; as Earl Temple he had been viceroy in 1782 and during his short administration he had discovered and punished several flagrant examples of peculation, which had not altogether increased his popularity. In June 1788 King George III was fifty and during the months that followed he suffered from a series of apparently minor complaints. From October onwards he was obviously ill and on 10 November Pitt was informed that the king's physicians considered: 'that His

Majesty's understanding is at present so affected that there does not appear to them any interval in which any act that he could do could properly be considered as done with a consciousness and understanding of what it was about'.

The king was essential to the government of the country and this was an unprecedented situation. Some action, therefore, had to be taken, but whatever action was taken was inevitably going to be of doubtful legality. All were agreed that the obvious regent was the prince of Wales, differences arose over his assumption and exercise of the royal power, namely: was it absolute and automatic, or limited and granted by parliament? In addition the Irish parliament was concerned with another issue; whether the Dublin parliament had an independent right to elect a regent during the king's illness, regardless of the action taken under these circumstances in England, and whether, if they legally possessed this right, it was expedient for them to exercise it. The Attorney-General, John Fitzgibbon, pointed out that the Act of Henry VIII, confirmed at the Revolution Settlement in 1692, which declared that 'this land of Ireland is depending and belonging . . . to the imperial crown of England', still stood on the statute book, and that this Act had been endorsed, rather than altered, in 1782. Nevertheless, assessing the situation, the Irish opposition decided that this was the occasion on which to emphasise the rights of the independent Irish parliament, accordingly they pressed their real or supposed claims to the utmost and disregarded the question of expediency.

This difficult situation was further complicated by the well-known antipathy which existed between the prince of Wales and his father. This mutual dislike and misunderstanding had led to the prince's friendship with the parliamentary opposition in England, and it was consequently anticipated that his assumption of the regency would automatically be followed by extensive ministerial changes. It was expected that these would inevitably result in the recall of the viceroy and that a new Lord Lieutenant nominated by the opposition, when they assumed office, might be expected to dismiss the political and confidential servants of his predecessors, and to transfer the favours and offices at the disposal of the Castle to the members of the Irish opposition.

Under these circumstances the solid phalanx of place-men wavered and many deserted. This defection shook to its foundation the system of the Castle bridging the gap between the executive and the legislature by creating political cohesion through a distribution of pension and place, and it underlined the problem which the commercial negotiations had revealed. The crisis ended as abruptly as it began, for by February 1789 the king had fully recovered. However, in a rush of enthusiasm to exercise their rights and liberties the Irish opposition, following a proposal by Grattan and ignoring the cautious legal exposition of the constitution offered by Fitzgibbon, had prepared an address requesting the prince of Wales to assume the regency of Ireland immediately and with full and unrestricted powers. On 18 February 1789 both Houses of Parliament, headed by the chancellor, Lord Lifford, and the speaker, John Foster, processed to the Castle to present the Address to the viceroy for transmission to the prince of Wales. Lord Buckingham declined to receive it: 'I cannot', he informed them, 'consider myself warranted to lay before the prince of Wales an address purporting to invest his Royal Highness with power to take on him the government of this realm before he shall be enabled by law so to do.' Highly displeased, the members of parliament returned to their respective Houses and Grattan moved a resolution to censure the viceroy and arrange a deputation to carry over their address to London.

Determined to uphold their dignity Grattan then moved a second resolution to the effect that the parliament of Ireland had exercised an undoubted right; to this Fitzgibbon, with considerable courage in view of the state of the House, rose to speak to the debate, advising 'the gentlemen of Ireland that the only security by which they hold their property, the only security they have for the present Constitution in Church and State, is the connexion of the Irish Crown with, and its dependence upon, the Crown of England . . . If they are not duped into idle and fantastical speculations under the pretence of asserting national dignity and independence, they will feel the effects to their sorrow. For give me leave to say, sir, that when we speak of the people of Ireland, it is a melancholy truth that we do not speak of the great body of the people. This is a subject on which it is painful to me to be obliged to touch in this assembly; but when I see the right honourable member driving the gentlemen of Ireland to the verge of a precipice, it is time to speak out . . . Sir, the ancient nobility of this kingdom have been hardly treated. The Act by which most of us hold our estates was an Act of violence – an Act subverting the first principles of the Common Law in England and Ireland. I speak of the Act of Settlement; and that gentlemen may know the extent . . . I will tell them that every acre of land which pays quit rent to the Crown is held by title derived under the Act of Settlement. So I trust gentlemen . . . will deem it worthy of consideration how far it may be prudent to pursue the successive claims of dignified and unequivocal independence made for Ireland by the right honourable gentleman . . . If the address of both Houses can invest the Prince of Wales with Royal power in this country, the same address could convey the same power to Louis XVI, or to his Holiness the Pope, or to the right honourable mover of this resolution . . . We are committing ourselves against the law and against the Constitution, and in such a contest Ireland must fall.' Possibly part of the reason for Fitzgibbon's unpopularity with the opposition was that he pointed out their fears, and in the acknowledgement of them, they hated him.

Secure in a common agreement by which they bound themselves to keep together and make government impossible should the king recover and the viceroy attempt to deprive any of them of office, the deputation left to present the Irish parliament's address to the prince of Wales in person. In their absence the opposition continued to harass the government in an endeavour to force the resignation of the Lord Lieutenant, fearing his retaliation should he not be recalled. The delegation arrived in London on 25 February 1789. On the same day the Irish House of Commons voted a short money bill. Five days later the viceroy received official confirmation that the king had fully recovered. Buckingham hastened to reassert his authority. The opposition's 'round-robin' proved useless when the viceroy divided them by offering an amnesty to those who would accept it. Originally these included Lord Shannon who had married Catherine Ponsonby; however, when he made overtures to the Castle she 'raved like a mad woman at her husband's desertion of her brother'. Mindful of his 'domestic quiet' Lord Shannon reluctantly remained in opposition. Consequently he lost the support and patronage of the government in the 1790 election for County Cork. The 2nd Duke of Leinster and William Ponsonby, who had gone to England with the address, were among those who had refused to make overtures to the viceroy and they were dismissed from their offices.

In June 1789 the opposition formed the Whig Club, which had the negative policy of preserving to Ireland 'in all time to come a Parliament of her own, residing within the realm and exclusively invested with all parliamentary privileges and powers' and the positive aim of the internal reform of that parliament. On the resignation of Lord Lifford, who died almost immediately afterwards, Fitzgibbon was appointed to succeed him as Lord Chancellor. Lord Mornington considered that among the major tasks of the Whig Club was 'the labour of answering the Chancellor's invectives'! This is not entirely fair, as, although there possibly was an almost personal attitude in their enmity to Fitzgibbon, nevertheless, they embarked on a reform movement aimed at the reduction of pensions and places and Catholic enfranchisement. However, the events of 1789 had made it obvious that this system of government could not long continue even without the extraordinary pressures exerted upon it by the unforeseen events of the 1790s. During the regency crisis Fitzgibbon had clearly told the House of Commons that, 'the only security of your liberty is your connection with Great Britain, and the gentlemen who risked breaking the connection must make up their minds to a union'.

7 Conclusion:
The Decade of Rebellion and the
Act of Union, 1790–1800

THE closing decade of the eighteenth century in Ireland unfolds with something of the powerful inevitability of a Greek tragedy. The unsolved problems of the century, the position of the ascendancy, the structure of government and the separatism of the Catholic majority all become enmeshed and move towards a climax against the ideological background of the French Revolution and the strategic implications of a major European war. Probably no event since the sack of Rome produced the cataclysmic effect upon European society equal to the impact of the French Revolution; and the horror and terror with which its progress was regarded, even in countries as fundamentally stable as England, was unsurpassed by any event in modern times. It is not surprising, then, that if the politically influential classes in England shuddered, the political ascendancy in Ireland, ever fearful of the immense Catholic majority and ever conscious of their hostility, were terrified, particularly in a situation over which they came to have increasingly less control: 'we are all afraid of the guillotine' wrote one prominent official in 1794. At the same time, the forces which were to erode the nascent prosperity of the country were already in operation, namely, the unprecedented growth in the population and the developing industrial revolution in England, whose consequences, by comparison, could not otherwise than adversely affect overpopulated, agrarian Ireland when the temporary war boom ceased. Thus the Indian summer of the closing decades of the Irish parliament gave to the nineteenth century a pernicious legacy of retrospective confusion between economic and political facts to link with the separatism of Catholic Irish nationalism which was the ultimate product of the '98 rebellion.

The 1790s were a period of chaotic development, which can be more easily understood if some of the closely entwined issues of these years are separated out, particularly: the position of the Catholics; the connection between the French Revolution and the United Irishmen; the views of Grattan and the parliamentary opposition; the problems of the Irish administration and the Fitzwilliam debâcle; and the conservative attitude of the majority of the ascendancy. The composite picture is one of all of these issues relating to and reacting upon each other with the French Revolution acting as a catalyst.

As the eighteenth century progressed the concept of religious toleration, reflected in Grattan's resolutions at the Dungannon Volunteer Convention in 1782, became increasingly accepted by educated English opinion, which was widely influenced by the deism of the age and the views of the French philosophers such as Voltaire and Rousseau. Toleration was also encouraged by more practical considerations. By the Peace of Paris in 1763 Great Britain had acquired and subsequently retained Canada and certain West Indian islands in which the population was predominently Catholic. In the treaty it was expressly stated that 'His Britannick Majesty agrees, on his side, to grant to the inhabitants of the countries above ceded, the liberty of the Catholic religion; he will, consequently, give the most express and the most effectual orders that his new Roman Catholick subjects may profess the worship of their religion according to the rites of the Romish church, as far as the laws of Great Britain permit.' This clause was very liberally interpreted on the political side where, for example, Roman Catholics were allowed into the Council of Grenada immediately following the peace and despite the objections of the newly arrived Protestants. By the 1790s British ministers, such as Grenville, felt very strongly that the behaviour of Great Britain towards her Catholic subjects in Canada and in Ireland was inconsistent, and this more tolerant outlook was expressed in the British Catholic Relief Act of 1791.

Encouraged by this more liberal atmosphere and by the parliamentary support of Grattan and various opposition groups like the Ponsonbys, the Catholic Committee again pressed for further relief. In 1790 they prepared a petition to parliament, but neither this nor an address to the new Lord Lieutenant, Lord Westmorland, produced any effect. During 1791 there was a power-struggle inside the Catholic Committee. The democratic elements triumphed and in October 1791, the month in which the United Irishmen were born, the Committee issued a forcible declaration demanding the abolition of the penal code. Conscious of the desirability of Protestant consent as well as acquiescence they pointed out that: 'objects material in their day produced hostility between our ancestors. The causes of that discord have ceased to exist; let the enmity too perish . . . We desire only that property in our hands may have its rational weight and merit in our children its rational encouragement'.

Meanwhile, the radical spirit engendered by the French Revolution was causing increasing alarm to the conservative elements in the administration and in parliament. Lord Lieutenant Westmorland shared their alarm and only consistent pressure from Pitt and Henry Dundas, the Secretary for the Southern Department, persuaded the Castle to support the very moderate measure of Catholic Relief introduced by Sir Hercules Langrishe early in 1792. Dundas even pointed out 'that the Roman Catholics will take the first favourable moment to extort by force what is denied to them as a matter of grace'. Nevertheless, during the debates, the Catholic Committee was very severely censured by the reluctant M.P.s, who thereby deprived the measure of any ameliorating qualities it might have possessed.

Angry and dissatisfied, the Catholic Committee proceeded to follow the example of the Volunteers during the last decade. A Convention of 300 delegates elected by electors chosen from every parish was summoned to meet at the Tailors' Hall in Back Lane in order to draw up a petition to the king stating their grievances. This petition by-passed the Castle and was presented to the king early in 1792 by representatives of the Convention led by John Keogh. The Catholic delegates were well received in London. As war drew imminent, the British ministers brought further pressure on the Irish administration; and, despite the fears of the ascendancy which increased as the French reign of terror gained momentum, Chief Secretary Hobart introduced and secured the reluctant consent of the Irish parliament to the Catholic Enfranchisement Act of 1793. This Act, amid other concessions, gave the parliamentary franchise to all Catholics who were otherwise qualified, and only membership of parliament and a few specified offices were excluded from them. Nevertheless, the nature of the electoral system automatically placed considerable restrictions upon the franchise unaccompanied by representative reform. These concessions had been grudgingly offered and ungraciously given and the demand now arose for complete emancipation.

The changing outlook of the Catholic Committee during the early 1790s was reflected in the men they employed as secretary: Richard Burke, the opinionated and tactless son of an influential and able father; and Theobald Wolfe Tone, who stood for much that Edmund Burke abhorred, and was not beyond using his position to proselytise for the United Irishmen. Beyond a certain point, however, he was unable to push wealthy and conservative merchants like Byrne and Keogh; 'as for merchants,' he commented in January 1793, 'I began to see they are no great hand at revolutions'. If Tone deplored the conservative attitude of the Catholic merchants whose property would have been the immediate and vulnerable victim of the revolution he envisaged, Keogh was extremely suspicious of Tone's political views. These suspicions were well founded, as by 1792 Tone had definitely embarked on the republican and revolutionary career, which he pursued with increasing fervour following the dissolution of the Catholic Convention in 1793, when his services were rewarded with a gold medal and a gratuity of £1,500.

The groundwork for a radical, if not a revolutionary, movement was already partly laid. After the failure of the Volunteer movement for parliamentary reform in the 1780s, Napper Tandy, a Dublin radical, tried to rally and expand the more extreme elements of the Volunteers, and although his immediate success was restricted, he kept the movement alive and personally exercised a great influence over Dublin Corporation. In the North the writings of Rousseau and Paine were attracting wide audiences among the Presbyterian ministers and the educated laity. Tone, in July 1791, referred to 'Paine's book, the Koran of Belfescu [Belfast]', while no less than four Irish newspapers reprinted the *Rights of Man*. At the same time Tone commented that he had 'much conversation about the Catholics, and their committee, &c., of which they know wonderfully little at Belfescu'. On another occasion, although he was reluctant to see the significance of his comment, he remarks that the northern Dissenters 'have not come forward in support of Catholic Emancipation, *save only in Belfast*'. It was against this background that the United Irishmen, in its origins a middle-class movement, came into being in October 1791. It was more a native

168

expression of the French Revolution than the heir of either the Volunteers or the Catholic Committee.

Tone had wished for a military rather than a legal career. It is therefore interesting to note the verdict of his most illustrious military contemporary, Arthur Wellesley, M.P. for Trim 1791–5 and later Duke of Wellington, who declared that: 'Wolfe Tone was a most extraordinary man, and his history the most curious of those times'. Theobald Wolfe Tone combined a sincere patriotism with a romantic attachment to revolutions. He was an idealist capable of a considerable degree of self-deception, regarding facts, when they refused to fit into his schemes, as he wished them to be rather than as they were in actuality. For instance, his own religious views were such that he never understood, or wanted to understand, the deep gap which separated Catholic from Dissenter and which was only superficially bridged at a middle-class level by the United Irishmen. The sectarian riots between the Protestant Peep o' Day boys and the Defenders were much more of a 'grass-roots' reality than the sophisticated non-sectarian concepts of the United Irishmen. A skirmish between these two groups at a cross-roads in county Armagh, afterwards known as the 'Battle of the Diamond', was followed by the formation of the Orange Order in 1795, and it was the Orange Order rather than the United Irishmen that absorbed the major part of the old Volunteer movement in Ulster.

Tone's *Autobiography* contrasts his awareness of the evidence for these divisions with his refusal to admit their existence. In his memorial to the French government he declares, 'that there is a certainty of a perfect harmony and co-operation between these two great bodies, which constitute nine-tenths of the population of Ireland', although on other occasions he gives evidence of considerable friction between 'these two great bodies'. His attitude to revolution was similarly ambivalent, as is shown in his impressive speech to the court-martial which tried him on 10 November 1798. Addressing them, he declared: 'But I hear it said that this unfortunate country has been prey to all sorts of horrors. I sincerely lament it. I beg, however, it may be remembered that I have been absent four years from Ireland. To me these sufferings can never be attributed. I designed by fair and open war to procure the separation of the two countries. For open war I was prepared; but, if instead of that, a system of private assassination has taken place, I repeat, whilst I deplore it, that it is not chargeable on me. Atrocities, it seems, have been committed on both sides. I do not less deplore them; I detest them from my heart; . . . ' This slippery logic has given Irish terrorism a seemingly permanent cloak for action without responsibility.

The revolutionary and separatist tradition which stems from '98 is of great significance in the subsequent development of Irish history. It is impossible, within the confines of this chapter, to analyse the views and opinions of all the prominent United Irishmen, but Tone more than any other leader, even Lord Edward Fitzgerald, lies at the core of the philosophy of '98. He typifies that Irish combination of, on the one hand, personal charm, family loyalty and political idealism, greater than but not untinged by personal ambition, with, on the other hand, an almost total disengagement from the bloody, often vicious, consequences of inflicting that political idealism on a populace, which may only partially comprehend or even agree with, the theories for which they are compelled to suffer so ruthlessly. Tone, from whom this inheritance comes, possessed great powers of persuasion, a high intelligence combined with a remarkable blindness, and a restless, feckless charm which brought him considerable popularity with his contemporaries and which frequently deflected them from realising the seriousness of his intentions. For example, he writes in his journal for 9 November 1792: 'at court . . .

Exceeding good laughing. Mr Hutton [i.e. Tone] called *Marat*. Sundry barristers apply to him for protection in the approaching rebellion. Lawyer Plunket applies for Carton, which Mr Hutton refuses, inasmuch as the Duke of Leinster is his friend, but offers him Curraghmore, the seat of the Marquis of Waterford. This Mr Hutton does to have a rise out of Marcus Beresford, who is at his elbow listening. Great laughter thereat.' In this context it is perhaps interesting to learn Tone's own verdict of Marat, whom he considered to be one of the foremost heroes of the French revolution: 'Marat', he declares, 'whom I believe to have been a sincere enthusiast, incapable of feeling or remorse'.

Wolfe Tone's *Autobiography* contains an explicit description of his ambitions and the methods whereby he hoped to gain support for his views in the first instance. These were: 'To subvert the tyranny of our execrable Government, to break the connection with England, the never-failing source of all our political evils, and to assert the independence of my country – these were my objects. To unite the whole people of Ireland, to abolish the memory of all past dissensions, and to substitute the common name of Irishman in place of the denominations of Protestant, Catholic and Dissenter – these were my means' and it was to convert the Dissenters to his views (he despaired of the Anglicans) that he wrote his famous pamphlet, *An Argument on behalf of the Catholics of Ireland* published in September 1791.

Following the dissolution of the Catholic Convention in 1793, and bitterly disappointed by the conservative and anti-rebellious attitude of the leading Catholics, Tone, to whom religion was principally, if not entirely, a means to an end, pressed on with his revolutionary plans assisted by men like Thomas Russell, Samuel Neilson and Henry Joy McCracken in Belfast, and the Sheares brothers, Napper Tandy, and Hamilton Rowan in Dublin; Arthur O'Connor and Lord Edward Fitzgerald joined the movement in

1796. War with revolutionary France was declared in 1793, and early in 1794 the Committee of Public Safety was contemplating the old strategy of attacking England through Ireland. For France the importance of Ireland was principally strategic, although most of the French leaders would also have considered that the establishment of a republic, friendly to France, would provide an additional idealistic bonus to consolidate the strategic advantages of detaching Ireland from England. They were singularly badly informed about affairs in Ireland. A few years later, in 1796, Tone recorded: 'I believe I have satisfied Hoche that he will not meet with prodigious assistance from his Majesty's Lord High Chancellor of Ireland', and Hoche was not the only person whom Tone had to convince that Fitzgibbon was not a promising revolutionary!

Early in 1794 the Rev. William Jackson, an Anglican clergyman of Irish extraction who had settled in France, arrived in Ireland as a French agent to assess the situation and make contact with the United Irishmen. Tone assured Jackson 'that circumstances in Ireland were favourable to a French invasion'. 'I said', Tone stated in his *Autobiography,* 'that it would be a most severe and grievous remedy for our abuses, but that I saw no other . . . I was one of those who, seeing all the danger and horror of a contest, still thought the independence of the country an object worth risking all to obtain.' Government had been aware of Jackson's activities and he was taken into custody, as was Hamilton Rowan, who effected a dramatic escape. Eventually, Jackson was brought to trial but before sentence could be passed he managed to consume a quantity of arsenic, alleged to have been administered by his wife, and he died in the dock.

Realising that he would be incriminated, Tone astutely went to the authorities, declared his involvement and offered to go into exile in America. The Irish government accepted his offer without asking for either parole or for any form of assurance as to his future conduct, 'a circumstance', he notes, 'of which I was most sincerely glad', for he considered 'that, undoubtedly, I was guilty of a great offence against the existing Government; that, in consequence, I was going into exile; and that I considered that exile as a full expiation for the offence, and consequently felt myself at liberty, having made that sacrifice, to begin again on a fresh score'! He left Ireland for Philadelphia on 13 June 1795 and on 2 February 1796 he landed in France. From that moment he worked ceaselessly to persuade the French authorities to send a substantial expeditionary force to Ireland.

Not all of the United Irishmen travelled as speedily along the road to revolution as Tone, and, apart from the Catholic question, one of the issues which occupied the Society during 1793–4 was that of parliamentary reform. A 'complete and radical reform of parliament' had been among the earliest ambitions of the United Irishmen, but it was not until the end of 1792 that in response to a motion from Thomas Addis Emmet a committee of twenty-one was appointed to draw up a plan for consideration by the society. This was to be formulated from a number of separate plans, and among the ideas which these advocated were that 'it must be a representation of the people, that is, persons not property must be the rule of representation; not land but lives; not money but men'; voting by ballot, disapproved of by some of the Ulster members who felt that it was morally dubious; payment of M.P.s; manhood suffrage at 21 or even 18; biennial parliaments; elections to be restricted to one day only; 'a seat in parliament should be vacated, by taking a place or pension, by absence for a certain part of the session'. Other ideas were discussed and they, like these, show not only a mixture of idealism and detail but political views which were considerably in advance of those usually canvassed during the eighteenth century. However, many of these ideas were not unique to the United Irishmen; the Society of the Friends of the People supported by Fox and Grey in England shared some of them, as did the Irish opposition led by Grattan and Ponsonby, who in December 1792 formed a society known as the Friends of the Constitution, Liberty and Peace.

This society, which was modelled on the Friends of the People in England, was founded by the leading members of the Whig Club as an alternative to the more radical United Irishmen. Their objectives were to maintain a hereditary monarchy, an assembly of nobles emanating from the Crown, and a body of representatives chosen by the people. These they held to be the vital parts of the constitution. At the same time they maintained that the permanent peace and welfare of Ireland required the abolition of all civil and religious distinctions and a radical reform of parliament. Catholic Emancipation and parliamentary reform were the dominant preoccupations of the Irish parliamentary opposition prior to 1797 when, like Fox and Grey in Great Britain, Grattan and some of his supporters seceded from the Irish House of Commons. 'The reason why we seceded was, 'declared Grattan, 'that we did not approve of the conduct of the United Men, and we could not approve of the conduct of the Government. We were afraid of encouraging the former by making speeches against the latter, and we thought it better in such a case as we could support neither to withdraw from both.' The 1790s were not propitious years for the moderate constitutional reformers who wished to keep a balance between the reactionary conservative and the incipient revolutionary.

The British opposition included both the conservative views of the followers of Portland and the more radical ones of the adherents of Fox. Under the impact of the French revolution these groups split. In 1794 the Portland group which had been moving steadily towards the government, especially after the outbreak of war in 1793, joined in a coalition with Pitt's administration. In the ensuing reorganisation the Duke of Portland went to the Home Office and Earl Fitzwilliam was appointed Lord Lieutenant of Ireland. Fitzwilliam had inherited great estates from his uncle, the second Marquis of Rockingham. In view of his property and family tradition Fitzwilliam enjoyed a prominent position in the Whig party, which it was felt entitled him to hold important office despite his lack of previous administrative experience. Grattan and the Ponsonbys, who had been disappointed in 1789, naturally rejoiced at the imminent arrival of a sympathetic viceroy and prospect of exercising great influence, and, in the case of Ponsonby, high position. Fitzwilliam encouraged these hopes.

It is not improbable that the foundations of Pitt's Irish policy were laid during the viceroyalty of the Duke of Rutland, 1784–7, when he and Rutland as young men contemplated the nature of Irish government at the time of the commercial negotiations: 'I believe', Pitt wrote to Rutland in August 1785, 'the time will yet come when we shall see all our views realised in both countries, and for the advantage of both. It may be sooner or later, as accident, or, perhaps, (for some time), malice may direct, but it will be right at last. We must spare no human exertion to bring forward the moment as early as possible, but we must be prepared also to wait for it on one uniform and resolute ground, be it ever so late.' In November 1792 Pitt was writing to Lord Lieutenant Westmorland that, 'the idea of the present fermentation, gradually bringing both parties to think of a union with this country, has long been in my mind. The admission of the Catholics to a share of suffrage would not then be dangerous.' In view of subsequent events it is important to try to assess Pitt's view of Irish affairs when Fitzwilliam was appointed. Portland from his long political experience and personal knowledge of Irish government may have had some realisation of Pitt's ultimate intentions, but it is very unlikely that Fitzwilliam had any information about, or intuition concerning, the British prime minister's long-term plans for the government to which he was so anxious to be appointed. It is equally unlikely that the inexperienced Fitzwilliam would have been Pitt's choice of a viceroy at this critical juncture. Fitzwilliam's appointment was a concession to the consolidation of the coalition government in the face of a major European war.

Shortly after his arrival in 1784 Rutland had written to Pitt stating that: 'a fixed and systematic plan should be determined upon in Cabinet for the future government of Ireland . . . A government whose schemes extend no further than the exigencies of the day cannot expect any decisive good effects from its measures.' There is no reason to believe that a major change was envisaged when Earl Fitzwilliam was appointed to the viceroyalty of Ireland, and there is considerable evidence to the contrary. It was not part of the coalition agreement concerning which Portland wrote to Fitzwilliam that 'the basis and sine quâ non condition must be the Re-establishment of Order and Good Government in France'. Nevertheless, the behaviour of both Portland and Fitzwilliam when the appointment became probable was certainly such as to encourage the aspirations of their friends in the Irish opposition. Portland wrote 'immediately to Ponsonby, but haven't had an opportunity yet of talking to Pitt upon it, you will suppose consequently that I have not mentioned it to the King'. Shortly after Fitzwilliam wrote to the same effect to Grattan, whom he had never met, adding that: 'it is, sir, to you and your friends, the Ponsonbys, that I look for assistance . . . Without the hope, which I am vain enough to entertain of that assistance, I should decline engaging in so hopeless a task as the government of Ireland.' The consequence of these communications was to cause such a ferment in Ireland that Pitt was forced to exert his authority. He wished to cancel the appointment of Fitzwilliam, but Fitzwilliam's pride was now involved and Portland and Windham both brought pressure to bear on Pitt to continue the appointment. At the same time they attempted to explain the nature of the viceregal office to Fitzwilliam, who then complained to Windham that his appointment had been made conditional: 'the conditions are that I slip into Ld. Westmorland's old Shoes . . . the men and measures are to be the same without any regard to my approbation or disapprobation.' Subsequently a general statement of policy along these lines was hammered out between Grattan, Burke, Fitzwilliam and the British Chancellor, Lord Loughborough. Pitt authorised Lord Westmorland to announce that there would be no change of policy in Ireland. To make assurance doubly sure a cabinet meeting was held before Fitzwilliam's departure to discuss in detail the policy to be followed by the viceroy on his arrival in Ireland. Certainly no Lord Lieutenant ever set out with more explicit instructions and none more speedily and totally disregarded them. Fitzwilliam never realised that the viceroy administered but did not rule the country; he was not a regent invested with the royal executive power but a channel for government. All his contemporaries were agreed that he was an honest man and given the truth of this assumption the only apparently viable conclusion is that he had so little comprehension of his office that he considered the government's careful instructions as advice to be disregarded, rather than commands to be obeyed. After his recall, in 1795, Speaker Foster, who strongly opposed the viceroy's Catholic policy declared him to be 'the weakest, well-meaning good man I have met'.

Fitzwilliam arrived in Ireland on Sunday, 4 January 1795. The day following his arrival he was indisposed and confined to his room. On Wednesday he dismissed John

Beresford, First Commissioner of the Revenue, on un-specified and unproven charges of maladministration: subsequently Fitzwilliam admitted that these charges 'arose from impressions he had received from those he had conversed with'. Beresford had served twenty-five years on the Revenue Board and the method of his dismissal was as peremptory as it was unjust. It was also illegal, as Pitt reminded or more probably informed Fitzwilliam that 'the change which has been thus announced, could never take effect but by direct authority from hence, and that under the signature of the Lords of the Treasury'.

Further dismissals rapidly followed. On 15 January, the heads of the civil and military departments of the Castle secretariat, Sackville Hamilton and Edward Cooke, were dismissed; 'a thousand reasons which I cannot detail', wrote Fitzwilliam, 'have compelled me to make up my mind to this measure.' At the same time the Attorney and Solicitor-General were informed that their removal was imminent as the Lord Lieutenant required their offices for George Ponsonby and John Curran respectively. Thus within a fortnight of his arrival Fitzwilliam had removed most of the leading officials in the government of Ireland, with one particular exception, the formidable Lord Chancellor, Lord Fitzgibbon. Grattan had informed Dr O'Beirne, Fitzwilliam's private secretary and later Bishop of Meath, that the removal of Fitzgibbon was an essential preliminary to his joining the administration. However, the Ponsonbys, perhaps wiser in the ways of government, advised against it, and when the idea reached the ears of the British cabinet it was specifically and emphatically for-bidden.

Every surviving viceroy for the previous thirty years regardless of his political affiliations protested against these dismissals. The officials concerned considered that their summary dismissals reflected on their personal and professional integrity, and wrote accordingly to their friends in England, pointing out their long and faithful services in a series of letters, which were on the whole both dignified and restrained. 'Mr Hamilton', wrote Edward Cooke to the Marquis of Buckingham, 'had merely fifty years of the most laborious and faithful service to plead, under all Administrations, whether adverse to each other or combined', while Beresford stated, 'if any one reason for displacing me can be produced, save only that I have supported Government . . . I am ready to resign'. By 1795 the Irish administrative officials felt that they owed their allegiance to 'English government' rather than to the transient person of the viceroy, therefore they could only be dismissed for incompetence or dereliction of duty, as, for instance, C. F. Sheridan had been dismissed from the Military Department in 1789 for refusing to support in parliament the government of which he was an administrative official. Even the opposition while declaring Beresford 'an English slave' added that 'in private he was an honourable man', while Fitzgibbon was admitted to possess 'a heart not quite devoid of every feeling of humanity'. Perhaps part of the difficulty lay then, as subsequently, in the curious ability of Irishmen to separate a man's private and public capacities in such a way that he can be an 'honourable gentleman' in one sphere and an insincere 'English slave' or 'Irish incendiary' in another; for political opponents to 'honourably disagree' has always been more difficult to accept.

The nature of the Irish legislature and its necessary but tenuous connection with Irish government made a degree of executive continuity essential for administrative stability, otherwise every variation in British politics would have reduced the government of Ireland to chaos. Fitzwilliam, on the other hand, had been brought up in the conservative Whig tradition and he did not realise the emergence of this convention. The Whigs had been in opposition for more than a decade. During that time the problems of administration probably tended to become distant and vague, while responsible and experienced criticism of government policy must on occasions have given way to the less responsible variety which provides an easy and safe pastime for a permanent opposition. The activities of these years possibly influenced Fitzwilliam, whose confidence and assurance never wavered throughout. He viewed his position and administration in an entirely personal light: 'immediately on my arrival', he wrote to Pitt, 'I took into consideration the measures that were most likely to give strength and credit to my administration', and when he was recalled he felt that 'to get rid then of me personally, and thereby to consign me over to immediate disgrace, has been the motive to everything that has happened relative to Ireland'. Even Burke reacted against Fitzwilliam's attitude to those who had been his friends: 'I am vexed too', he wrote to Grattan, 'that when Windham, who . . . did everything that a man could do to heal the breach, had written to Lord Fitzwilliam, his answer had been so very cold and repulsive . . . There never was a more exalted mind than that of Lord Fitzwilliam, – exalted are irritable minds', and not always practical ones.

Turning from men to measures, Fitzwilliam regarding the policy to be adopted by his administration, seems to have felt a similar liberty to abrogate his previous engagements. At the cabinet meeting prior to his departure, 'the conversation turned to the course to be pursued respecting the public measures, on which it was understood that on all important subjects Lord Fitzwilliam should transmit all the information he could collect, with his opinion, to the King's servants here, and that he should do nothing to commit the King's Government . . . without fresh instructions from hence. It is also distinctly recollected by some of the persons present that the Catholic question was particularly mentioned . . . the same principles before stated were considered as applying to this . . . a strong opinion was stated that Lord Fitzwilliam should, if possible, prevent the agitation of the question at all during the present Session.' Fitzwilliam had been in Ireland little more than a week when he wrote to Portland, stating that, 'it is my opinion, that *not to grant cheerfully* on the part of Government all the Catholics wish, will not only be exceedingly impolitick, but *perhaps dangerous*'. The Lord Lieutenant's argument was that the substance of power had already been granted by the Catholic Enfranchisement Act of 1793. This Act had completed the concessions given in the Acts of 1778, 1782 and 1792, consequently the Catholics were now excluded from only a very few specified positions. At the same time, the state of the French war made invasion highly probable, and under these circumstances national unity was essential. The only way to acquire this unity was by granting total Catholic Emancipation and making 'the people of Ireland *one People*'.

The British ministry displayed their customary dilatoriness in replying to the viceroy's despatch. In the interim Fitzwilliam allowed Grattan to obtain leave from the House of Commons to introduce a bill granting Catholic Emancipation before the British ministers had seen a draft of the proposed measure or even approved the idea. This unprecedented behaviour on the part of the viceroy caused consternation among his colleagues and friends in England and Fitzwilliam had not been seven weeks in Ireland when the Duke of Portland wrote on 21 February 1795 to inform him that '. . . the cause of Government abstractly considered, requires that you should not continue to administer that of Ireland'. Portland continues his letter referring to Grattan's desire for popularity and the influence that it 'may have in his attachment to many political schemes in which he has been engaged', – this was probably unfair as Grattan realised and was profoundly concerned about the diverse effect of religion in preventing the unity of the peoples of Ireland and the development of an Irish nation.

Portland further indicated that while acknowledging the benefits of 'Mr Ponsonby's influence . . . I can not overlook the magnitude & extent of his expectations, nor that original taint which has affected too many of us Whigs in our feelings for the established Church . . .' and he also disapproved of Fitzwilliam's judicial dismissals and the 'avowal of distrust' implicit in the dismissal of Sackville Hamilton and Edward Cooke. He concluded his comprehensive indictment by censuring the viceroy's consent to Grattan's motion for leave to introduce the Catholic Bill before the ministry had approved it.

These were the reasons for Fitzwilliam's recall, and they were essentially administrative rather than political. Fitzwilliam had failed to obey the unwritten conventions of his office as they had been indicated to him on more than one occasion before he embarked upon it. Nevertheless, Fitzwilliam, who consistently showed an almost total blindness towards the machinery through which Ireland was governed, never realised that he had overturned the machine, any more than he understood the total disruption which his administrative dismissals created. Even his friends were forced, reluctantly and regretfully, to admit that despite his personal virtues he had no comprehension whatsoever of the nature of his office or the complexity of its administration. It is difficult to estimate the extent of the repercussions of this disastrous event upon subsequent Anglo-Irish relations, probably its most serious consequence was that premature agitation for Catholic Emancipation turned the already uneven mind of George III against it. The royal consent was still an essential element in British politics, and by creating a situation in which the king's mind was already made up beyond persuasion, Fitzwilliam's good intentions destroyed any prospect of success for the Act of Union.

The Catholic question was one of peculiar delicacy, and the ramifications of it are not always easy to understand today. As Portland's comments on 'that original taint which has affected too many of us Whigs in our feelings for the established Church' indicates it was not an entirely Irish issue – where natural justice and national unity pulled one way and the fears of the ascendancy pulled another – and it is perhaps more comprehensible when viewed in its wider context. It was considered that the British constitution as guaranteed by the Bill of Rights and the Act of Settlement rested on the fact that 'it is inconsistent with the safety and welfare of this Protestant Kingdom to be governed by a Popish Prince'. Thus the British crown and the Hanoverian succession were inextricably bound up with the support and maintenance of the Church of England. This situation was automatically extended, not only to Ireland but to all Britain's overseas dependencies, for example, although there was a definite shortage of white settlers and men of sufficient education to hold office in the Leeward Islands, an 'Act to admit upon conditions, white persons professing the Roman Catholic religion in the Leeward Islands, to all the Rights and Privileges enjoyed by Protestant subjects within the same' which was passed by the legislature and warmly supported by the acting Governor on the grounds that the 'Roman Catholics were very faithful and loyal subjects' was nevertheless disallowed in 1799 when it came before the British Privy Council. Some idea of this concept of the interdependence between the Church and State establishments can be seen in George III's attitude to the rejection of a motion to alter the English Test and Corporation Acts in 1787. On this occasion the king declared to Pitt that 'every friend to good order must feel rejoiced'. When he heard of a suggestion that some provision should be made by the State for the Catholic clergy of Ireland he indicated that 'such an idea must give real offence to the established Church in Ireland as well as to the true friends of our constitution'.

The issue of Catholic Emancipation was to divide

successive British administrations, – always more liberal than the majority of the Irish ascendancy – for over a generation and the final passing of Catholic Emancipation in 1829 was to be among the most schismatic events in British politics. Whether, against this background, Catholic Emancipation could have been passed by the Irish parliament during the 1790s remains debatable, especially in view of the attitude of many M.P.s expressed in the debates in 1792 and 1793 and the powerful opposition of men like Speaker Foster. The Act of Union, with the precedent of the guarantees given to the Scottish Church in 1707, undoubtedly offered the best opportunity but this was lost probably in part at least through the well intentioned efforts of Grattan and Fitzwilliam in 1795. The bill which Grattan had introduced in February 1795, during Fitzwilliam's viceroyalty, was defeated by 155 to 84 votes in the following May.

Fitzwilliam was succeeded in March 1795 by the Earl of Camden. Camden was a political associate of Pitt and his Chief Secretary, Thomas Pelham, belonged to Portland's circle. Pelham had previously been Chief Secretary to Lord Northington in 1783, so he had experience of Ireland in addition to a considerable reputation for political ability. Unfortunately his health was poor and consequently he spent a considerable part of his period of office in England. His duties gradually passed to Camden's nephew Robert Stewart, Lord Castlereagh, who officially succeeded Pelham in March 1798. Camden, a man of only moderate abilities and largely deprived of his Chief Secretary's experience and advice, inherited a difficult situation which became steadily worse. He took fright and allowed himself to be pressured by the reactionary views of the majority of the equally frightened ascendancy.

The government was anxious to conciliate Catholic hopes, which recent events had brought to the highest pitch, and which had been correspondingly disappointed by the Fitzwilliam debâcle. One of the consequences of the French revolution had been the closure of the Irish colleges in France where most of the Catholic clergy and some of the laity had been educated, while the outbreak of war had made access to colleges in other Catholic countries difficult. As an immediate response to this need St Patrick's College, Carlow, had been established in 1793, but there was an obvious need for further provision, and as a gesture of conciliation the government established the Royal College of St Patrick at Maynooth. Although Maynooth College was to become one of the most influential educational establishments in the Catholic world, it failed to achieve its immediate objective – the pacification of disappointed Catholic political ambitions, for the background against which it was created had developed beyond such palliatives.

As early as May 1794 the government had become seriously alarmed by the activities of the United Irishmen and the Society had been officially suppressed. This had the effect of driving it underground where, under the influence of Tone and others, it turned increasingly towards the idea of an alliance with revolutionary France – a scheme which Tone put all his energies into forwarding when he went into exile in June 1795 and arrived in France *via* America in February 1796. His powers of persuasion must have been very considerable as he not only succeeded where others failed, notably Lord Edward Fitzgerald, but he also surmounted the linguistic barrier, with which he confessed he was ill-equipped to cope. He persuaded Carnot and the French Directory to second an able general, Hoche, and to yield to their combined persuasion to assign adequate troops and equipment for the expedition which the Directory were not at first willing to do. Nevertheless Hoche persisted: 'men will not sacrifice themselves when they do not see a reasonable prospect of support;' telling Tone 'but, if I go, you may be sure I will go in sufficient force', and the expedition which set sail from Brest in

December 1796 comprised approximately 15,000 men in 43 ships of which 17 were ships of the line.

Hoche appears to have taken some trouble to get to know Tone and also to inform himself about the state of Ireland. His first concern was naturally about the availability of provisions: 'when he mentioned his anxiety as to bread, Carnot laughed, and said, "There is plenty of beef in Ireland; if you cannot get bread, you must eat beef." I told him I hoped they would find enough of both; adding, that within the last twenty years Ireland had become a great corn country, so that at present it made a considerable article in her exports.' An interesting comment on the fame of Ireland's provision trade, as well as on the development of tillage which was so noted a feature of Irish agriculture during the late eighteenth century, especially following the encouragement given by Foster's Corn Law in 1784.

Hoche was also interested in the political state of the country, for instance he enquired of Tone: 'who are those Orange-boys?'. It is possible that he was not unaware of the element of wishful thinking in Tone's assessment of the religious situation: 'he then asked me', Tone recollected, 'what I thought of the priests . . . I replied I certainly did not calculate on their assistance, but neither did I think they would be able to give us any effectual opposition . . . in prudence we should avoid as much as possible shocking their prejudices unnecessarily . . . I was satisfied it would be absolutely impossible for them to take the people out of our hands'; the converse of this statement did not occur to Tone.

Beyond a vague statement of republicanism, Tone's *Autobiography* gives no detail of the type of government envisaged should the rebellion have been successful. The various efforts made by the French to elicit further detail were unrewarding. Hoche, however, did point out to him that he considered that great harm had been done to the principles of liberty by the quantity of blood spilt during the French revolution: 'for', he added, 'when you guillotine a man you get rid of an individual, it is true, but then you make all his friends and connections enemies for ever to the Government'. 'A sentence', Tone remarks, 'well worth considering. I am heartily glad to find Hoche of this humane temperament, because I hope I am humane myself . . .'

While Tone was making arrangements for a French invasion, the situation continued to degenerate in Ireland. Sectarian violence and agrarian unrest grew stronger among the poorer sections of the community, while the proscribed United Irishmen pursued their revolutionary plans with increasing enthusiasm. Confronted with these dangers, the Irish parliament grew more reactionary and more repressive and the strength and influence of the opposition diminished. In their attitude the members of the Irish parliament were not alone as a similar wave of reaction, with less foundation, swept through the contemporary British parliament. In February 1796 an Insurrection Act made it a capital offence to administer an illegal oath, and gave the Lord Lieutenant and the Privy Council powers to proclaim a district that they considered to be disturbed; this proclamation gave the magistrates special powers of search and arrest. It was under the terms of this Act that the Ulster Presbyterian, William Orr, was executed. Some indication of the mind of the Irish parliament is shown by the division list of 157 to 7 on the suspension of the Habeas Corpus Act in November 1796. Nevertheless, Grattan and Ponsonby continued to bring before parliament the questions of Catholic emancipation and parliamentary reform, but any prospect of success in the foreseeable future became increasingly unlikely. It was when Ponsonby's attempt to introduce a reform bill, through a series of resolutions encompassing both parliamentary reform and Catholic emancipation failed, that the Irish opposition followed Fox's example at Westminster and in 1797 seceded from parliament. Their position had long been peculiarly difficult.

In September 1796 the government arrested Russell and Neilson along with other leaders of the Ulster section of the United Irishmen. Finally in December 1796 Hoche's long expected expedition sailed. It was too late in the year, for, although the flotilla escaped the watching British navy, it was subsequently scattered by violent gales. Many of the ships, including the one which carried Hoche, were blown out into the Atlantic and never came to Ireland at all. Part of the expedition, including Tone's section, did actually reach Bantry Bay but divisions among the command, and continued bad weather, prevented them from landing. Ultimately the various parts of the scattered expedition limped back to France, where the following September Hoche died.

During 1796, as the influence of the parliamentary opposition grew weaker, two M.P.s Arthur O'Connor, M.P. for Philipstown, and Lord Edward Fitzgerald, M.P. for Kildare, joined the United Irishmen. They had long shown republican sympathies and had previously tried and failed to influence the French in support of Irish radicalism. Tone, O'Connor and Fitzgerald were all born in the same year, 1763, so that although legend has given them perpetual youth they were in fact only four years younger than Pitt; however, only O'Connor survived to old age, dying in 1852, the same year as Wellington, who was six years younger. Lord Edward Fitzgerald was a cousin of Charles James Fox. His mother Emily, Duchess of Leinster, had believed in a liberal education for her children – she had contemplated Rousseau as a possible tutor. Lord Edward's personality had a greater share of charm and good nature than it had of intelligence. He had automatically imbibed the position of the Fitzgerald family as the natural leaders of Irish society. A younger son, Lord

Edward had entered the army during the American war, and naturally resented being subsequently cashiered from it for attending a revolutionary banquet in Paris as Citizen Fitzgerald. Returning home he had nearly been expelled from the House of Commons in 1793 for making derogatory remarks about the viceroy, Lord Westmorland. Nevertheless, he did not actually join the United Irishmen until 1796. Thereafter, he rose speedily in its hierarchy and became its military commander.

By the beginning of 1797 the country was in a state of suppressed rebellion. The danger was particularly severe in the North which still abounded in weapons left over from the Volunteer movement, while it was well known that additional weapons were being made in forges up and down the country. In March 1797 the government decided to disarm Ulster and the task was entrusted to General Lake, a limited and unimaginative soldier. Lake carried out his duties with a ruthless brutality that created both a seething resentment at the time, and an uneasy peace over much of the province for the remainder of the crisis period, for although attempts were made to encourage risings in the province in '98, notably by Henry Munro and Henry Joy McCracken, the sting had gone out of the rebellion in the North. This was a curious sequel considering that Ulster had originally provided the idealistic basis for the rebellion.

The reasons for this unexpected tranquillity were varied: firstly, timing, the crisis had continued for too long and the impetus had worn itself out; secondly, the underlying sectarianism, expressed in the rise of the Orange Order; thirdly, economic, the dependence of the country upon the linen trade which civil disturbance inevitably upset; fourthly, disenchantment with republican France and particularly with her foreign policy towards Switzerland and America. 'The Northerners', Pelham was informed in June 1798, 'do not like the Papists. They feel the injuries [of the French] to America. They have not the plenty of provisions the Wexfordians had. They possess the escheated counties; and their bleachers, though they would huckster with any man who would promise to govern them cheapest, will not like the destructions of their greens.' Perhaps there was also something in the Ulster temperament which contributed to this situation. Dean Warburton told Cooke, who was puzzled by 'the quiet of the North' that 'the cunning and wary Northerners see that no revolution can be effected without a foreign aid', while Camden pointed out to Portland 'that with their disaffection they join much prudence'.

The Castle had a number of informers, and in particular Thomas Reynolds. Reynolds joined the society in 1797 and shortly after he became a member of the Leinster provincial directory. In consequence of the information which they had received the administration decided to prevent the rising by arresting the members of the Leinster directory in March 1798. On this occasion, Lord Edward Fitzgerald escaped and remained in hiding until 19 May, when he was mortally wounded while evading arrest. Knowing that he was dying, his aunt, Lady Louisa Conolly, wished to visit him. She appealed in vain to the viceroy, Lord Camden, and then turned to Fitzgibbon, now Lord Clare, who told her that he could not give her such permission, but that he would immediately go with her to Lord Edward. Following the rebellion both Fitzgibbon and Castlereagh tried to exercise a moderating influence over the frightened and vengeful conservative elements in the ascendancy led, curiously, by Archbishop Agar of Cashel.

Despite the more liberal policies of General Abercromby and the repressive measures of General Lake, the incipient rebellion finally broke out in May–June 1798. The disarming of Ulster, the capture of the Leinster directory and finally the death of Lord Edward made it hopeless before it started. Without general direction it lacked co-ordination and it erupted in a series of sporadic outbursts. It was only widespread in the south-east where it took a definitely sectarian character before making a final stand at Vinegar Hill near Enniscorthy in County Wexford. The whole course of the rebellion was marked by that train of atrocity, treachery and bitterness that is the inescapable concomitant of civil war. Perhaps the final comment should be left with Tone himself: 'Atrocities, it seems have been committed on both sides . . . In a cause like this, success is everything. Success in the eyes of the vulgar fixes its merit.' Unfortunately defeat fixes its bitterness.

From the outbreak of the insurrection Tone had been urging the French government to act: 'the present crisis must be seized', he urged in June 1798, 'or it would be too late; that I could hardly hope the Irish, unprovided as they were of all that was indispensable for carrying on a war, could long hold out against the resources of England, especially if they saw France make no effort whatsoever to assist them . . . now was the moment to assist them: in three months it might be too late, and the forces then sent, if the Irish were overpowered in the meantime, find themselves unsupported, and in their turn, be overpowered by the English.' This is almost a precise picture of what actually happened. At the end of August 1798 a small French force under General Humbert landed in Connacht and, although the French forces attracted some local support, they were hopelessly outnumbered by the viceregal forces under the new Lord Lieutenant, Marquis Cornwallis, to whom Humbert surrendered in September 1798. At the beginning of October another small French expedition was captured in Lough Swilly, County Donegal. On the flag-ship *Hoche* was Wolfe Tone, with a commission as a serving French officer. He was brought to Dublin and tried by Court Martial, although he had never been in either the British or Irish armies and the civil courts were then sitting. In the course of the trial he committed suicide, dying on 19 November 1798.

Except for the abortive flicker of Emmet's rebellion in 1803, in consequence of which Tone's friend Russell, not long released from prison following his complicity with the United Irishmen, got involved and executed, the revolutionary and separatist movement went underground. The ordinary people of Ireland, the traditional victims of her civil wars, the ultimate sufferers for causes which they have frequently only partially comprehended, once again returned to their everyday life and the consolation of their Churches. Henceforth Irish republican nationalism has been largely sectarian in character, a situation which was forged in '98, cooled in the Act of Union and toughened by the political and economic events of the nineteenth century.

'We must wait times and seasons,' Pitt had told Rutland in 1785, and in 1792 he had written to Westmorland, 'a union with this country has long been in my mind.' The events of the 1790s culminating in the rebellion had hastened the plans which Pitt had hoped that time would mature. Thus the immediate background to the union was the product of exhaustion rather than of evolution, as in the aftermath of despair, uncertainty and bitterness the government once again looked at the old and apparently insoluble problems: the Anglo-Irish connection with its strategic, commercial and political overtones; the structure of the Irish administration with its uncertain and vulnerable foundations, revealed by the regency crisis and the Fitzwilliam episode; the nature of the Irish parliament and the question of parliamentary reform; the social and religious divisions among the Irish people which had been so recently highlighted in the atrocities of the rebellion. It was felt that only a radical approach could solve this impasse, and before the insurrection had died down plans for the Union were under way.

Wolfe Tone died on 19 November 1798; the speech from the throne on 22 January 1799 recommended 'some permanent adjustment, which may extend the advantages enjoyed by our sister kingdom to every part of this island'. Opposition was vehement and immediate. Among those most violently opposed to the idea were Sir John Parnell, the Chancellor of the Exchequer; the opposition leader, George Ponsonby; and Sir Lawrence Parsons. When the Address in reply to the king's speech came before the House, the clause advocating the Union was deleted by a division list of 111 to 106. However, Castlereagh was able and Pitt was determined, while Cornwallis' character and reputation commanded respect. During the ensuing year every strategem of management and weapon of propaganda were applied with the utmost skill. Availing itself of the terms of the Place Bill, which Forbes and the parliamentary opposition had fought so hard to obtain in 1793, government, in so far as it was able, rearranged the House. The influence of Speaker Foster, even the return of Grattan to political life, proved powerless and on 5 February 1800 both Houses of Parliament received from the Lord Lieutenant the king's recommendation for a legislative union, 'as it unquestionably is the common interest, of both his kingdoms'. Castlereagh introduced the debate on the king's message about 4 p.m. on the afternoon of 5 February and when the debate concluded at 1 p.m. the following day the message was agreed by a majority of 43 votes. The division on this occasion, 158 to 115, was said to have been the largest in the history of the Irish House of Commons. Lord Clare introduced the measure into the House of Lords, where the government had an easy majority of 75 to 26.

The Act of Union was accompanied by another Act compensating the disfranchised borough-proprietors. It is an interesting fact that the most highly compensated borough-proprietor, the Marquis of Downshire, who received £52,500, and the most highly compensated official, the Speaker of the House of Commons, John

Foster, were among the strongest opponents of the Union. Foster, far from being a rich man was in debt. His office had been nearly as expensive as it was honourable. Eighty boroughs were completely disfranchised by the Act of Union, and thirty-two others were reduced to one member each; only Dublin, Cork and the county constituencies retained the same representation in the imperial parliament of the United Kingdom as they had enjoyed in the parliament of Ireland.

The Anglo-Scottish Act of Union had been based upon a treaty between two co-equal kingdoms. Ireland's position was, as was frequently stated during the eighteenth century, that of a dependent kingdom, and as such slightly different, while the circumstances under which the Act was passed were completely different. The 1800 Act was based upon a series of articles; these were agreed by the Irish parliament on 28 March and by the British parliament on 12 May 1800. The agreed articles were then incorporated into a bill, which passed through both parliaments and received the royal assent on 1 August 1800. It became operative on 1 January 1801.

Although Pitt had been unable to accompany it with complete Catholic emancipation and resigned from office on this account, nevertheless, the bill did carry with it a measure of indirect parliamentary reform which was entirely beneficial to the Catholic voters who had been enfranchised by the 1793 Act. Under the terms of article four, which was concerned with detailing the representation from both Houses of parliament, the Irish counties dominated the Irish representation in the Westminster parliament, and it was in these constituences that the Catholic voter was strongest. The Act is a long and in places a complicated document, but other articles of particular interest are: article seven, which arranged that the common budget was to be met in the ratio of 15 parts from England and 2 from Ireland, previous national debts were to be kept separate as were the exchequers; article eight, which continued the legal systems as they were constituted in both countries; and article five which united the established Churches in both countries 'into one Protestant episcopal church, to be called, The United Church of England and Ireland'.

Considering the circumstances of both countries in 1800, these terms were not ungenerous. Pitt, among others, hoped that the union would be the beginning of a new Irish policy in which Irish issues could be resolved in the wider and more stable political atmosphere of the United Kingdom parliament. The untimely death of Pitt, the long struggle against Napoleon, and even the longevity of George III were all unexpected; though perhaps a more foreseeable element was the loyalty to the concept of the unity of church and state inherent in the Church of England establishment, – an idea that was alien to the mind of the Irish Catholic and Presbyterian alike, but a concept which for so long delayed Catholic emancipation. Even more importantly in 1800, England, like Ireland, was still essentially an agricultural country and the social and economic results of the industrial revolution were as unpredicted as were the rapidity of their impact and their political consequences. Another unexpected phenomenon was the astonishing growth in the population of both countries for, although it had already begun by 1800, it was only partially realised, and its implications were almost totally unrecognised.

The rapidity and the nature of the extraordinary changes of the nineteenth century, most of which reacted unfavourably upon Ireland, cannot justly be laid upon the legislators of the Act of Union, – despite their imperfections. It was the course of events, rather than the malevolent intention of politicians, which destroyed the apparent promise of the eighteenth century and gave the last years of the Irish parliament the retrospective glow of a golden age.

Bibliography

THOSE who wish to read beyond the confines of this selected bibliography will find further, and more detailed, information in T. W. Moody (ed.) *Irish historiography 1936–70* (Irish Committee of Historical Sciences, 1971) and E. M. Johnston, *Irish history: a select bibliography* (Historical Association, revised ed. 1972). Two general histories, now in paperback, give good surveys of the period and have excellent critical bibliographies: J. C. Beckett, *The Making of Modern Ireland* (1966) which includes a select list of books on local history while *The Course of Irish History*, ed. T. W. Moody and F. X. Martin (Cork 1967) has in addition a useful chronological table.

1. Primary sources in print. Many important collections of official and private papers have been published by the British and Irish governments. The government stationery offices in London, Dublin and Belfast can supply details about the publications of the three Public Record Offices; the Public Record Office, London (P.R.O.), the Public Record Office of Ireland (P.R.O.I.) and the Public Record Office of Northern Ireland (P.R.O.N.I.). H.M. Stationery Office, London, supplies two pamphlets, *Record Publications Sectional List No. 24* and *Publications of the Royal Commission on Historical Manuscripts, Sectional List No. 17*, which list British publications indicating price and availability.

Official publications: *Calendars of State Papers,*

1688–1715, Calendar of Home Office Papers, (Cal. H.O.P.), 1760–1776, 4 vols. Historical Manuscripts Commission Reports (H.M.C.): Emly, Donoughmore, Charlemont I & II, Rutland III, Carlisle, Fortescue I, II, III, Stopford-Sackville I, Lothian, Various Collections VI, Hastings IV. Irish Manuscripts Commission *(I.M.C.)*: B. Jennings (ed.), *The wild geese in Spanish Flanders;* M. Walsh (ed.), *Spanish knights of Irish origin,* (2 vols); J. Ainsworth (ed.), *Inchquin MSS;* E. MacLysaght (ed.), *Kenmare MSS;* B. Fitzgerald (ed.), *Correspondence of Emily, Duchess of Leinster* (3 vols.). P.R.O.N.I., H.M.S.O., Belfast, *Eighteenth century Irish official Papers in Great Britain; Lord Massereene; Aspects of Irish Social History, 1750–1800,* (ed.) W. H. Crawford and B. Trainor.

Printed collections of documents. Reference has been made to the following: *English Historical Documents,* vols VIII, X, XI (vol VIII, 1660–1714, ed. A. Browning; vol X, 1714–1783, ed. D. B. Horn and M. Ransome; vol XI 1783–1832, ed. A. Aspinall and E. A. Smith); W. C. Costain and J. Steven Watson, *The law and working of the constitution: Documents,* 1660–1714, 2 vols; C. Grant Robertson, *Select Statutes, Cases and Documents* (1935 ed.). *Memoirs and Correspondence*: Barrington, *Personal sketches of his own times,* J. Barrington, 3 vols (1832); Beresford, *Correspondence of the Rt. Hon. John Beresford,* ed. Rt. Hon. W. Beresford, 2 vols (1854); Boulter: *Letters,* 2 vols (Dublin 1770); Buckingham, *Courts and Cabinets of George III,* ed, 2nd Duke, 4 vols (1848); Burke, *Correspondence of Edmund Burke,* (ed.) T. Coupland (1958–f), esp. vols VIII & IX (ed. R. B. McDowell); Carleton, *Life of William Carleton: being his autobiography . . .* ed. and completed D. J. O'Donoghue, 2 vols (1896); Castlereagh, *Memoirs and correspondence of Viscount Castlereagh,* ed. 3rd Marquis of Londonderry, vols I–IV (1829); Charlemont, *Memoirs of the political and private life of James Caulfield, Earl of Charlemont,* F. Hardy, 2 vols (1812); Cornwallis,

Correspondence of Charles, 1st Marquis Cornwallis, ed. C. Ross, vols II & III (1859); Delany, *The autobiography and correspondence of Mary Granville, Mrs Delany*, ed. Lady Llandover (1st and 2nd series) 6 vols (1861–2); Eden, *Journal and Correspondence of William, Lord Auckland*, ed. Bishop of Bath and Wells, 4 vols (1861–2); Edgeworth (R.L.), *Memoirs begun by himself and concluded by his daughter, Maria Edgeworth*, 2 vols (1820); Flood, *Memoirs of the life and correspondence of the Rt. Hon. Henry Flood*, ed. Warden Flood (Dublin, 1838); Grafton, *Autobiography and correspondence of Augustus Henry, 3rd Duke of Grafton*, ed. W. R. Anson (1898); Grattan, *Memoirs of the life and times of the Rt. Hon. Henry Grattan, by his son*, Henry Grattan, 5 vols (1839–46); George III, *Correspondence of King George III, 1760–83*, ed. J. Fortescue, 6 vols, *1783–1820* ed. A. Aspinall, 2 vols; Grenville, *Additional Grenville Papers*, ed. J. R. G. Tomkinson (1962); Harcourt, *Harcourt Papers*, ed. W. E. Harcourt, vols IX & X (50 copies only, 1888–1905); Knox, *Extra Official State Papers*, ed. W. Knox (1789); Lennox, *Life and letters of Lady Sarah Lennox, 1745–1826*, ed. Countess of Ilchester, 2 vols (1901); Loveday (J.), *Diary of a tour in 1732 through parts of England, Wales and Scotland*, (Roxburghe Club 1890); King, *A great archbishop of Dublin, William King D.D. 1650–1729*, C. S. King (1906); Macartney, *Some account of the official life and a selection from the unpublished writings of the Earl of Macartney*, J. Barrow, 2 vols (1807); Orrery: *The Orrery Papers*, ed. Countess of Cork and Orrery, 2 vols (1903); Rockingham, *Memoirs of the Marquis of Rockingham and his contemporaries*, 6th Earl of Albemarle, 2 vols (1852); Rutland, *Correspondence between the Rt. Hon. William Pitt, and Charles, Duke of Rutland*, ed. John, Duke of Rutland (1890); Shelburne, *Life of William Earl of Shelburne*, Lord Edward Fitzmaurice, 3 vols (1875–6); Swift, *Correspondence of Jonathan Swift*, ed. H. Williams, 5 vols (Oxford 1963–5); *Prose Works*, ed. H. Davis, 14 vols (1939–68); Tone, *Life of Theobald Wolfe*

Tone . . . written by himself and continued by his son, ed. R. B. O'Brien, 2 vols (1893); Walpole, *Memoirs of the reigns of King George II, King George III, and Last Journals of the reign of King George III*, 8 vols (1822, 1894 and 1910 editions); Wesley, *The works of John Wesley* (Wesleyan Conference edition, 1872); Young (A.), *A tour of Ireland 1776–9*, ed. A. W. Hutton, 2 vols (1892). There is also a considerable amount of correspondence printed in Ashbourne, *Pitt, some chapters of his life and times* and Roseberry, *Pitt*.

2. Secondary authorities. W. E. H. Lecky, *History of Ireland in the eighteenth century*, 5 vols (1892). This classic history remains the outstanding work on this period; it is particularly valuable for its extensive quotations from original sources and his *Leaders of public opinion in Ireland* (1861 and 1871 editions) has essays on Swift, Flood and Grattan. Similar in vintage though not in quality is J. A. Froude, *The English in Ireland in the eighteenth century*, 3 vols (1881). Three books of essays contain useful studies on eighteenth-century topics: H. A. Cronne, T. W. Moody and D. B. Quinn eds.; *Essays in British and Irish history in honour of J. E. Todd* (1949) contains studies on Swift, the Irish viceroyalty 1760–73, the conflict between Flood and Grattan, and an eighteenth-century land agent; C. Litton Falkiner's *Essays relating to Ireland* (1907) has an essay on Archbishop Stone, while his *Studies in Irish history and biography* (1902) consider Lord Clare, the Earl-Bishop, and the French invasion of 1798.

(a) *Political and administrative*. J. G. Simms, *Jacobite Ireland, 1685–91* (1969) and *The Williamite confiscation in Ireland, 1690–1703* (1956); I. Ehrenpreis, *Swift: the man, his works and the age*, 3 vols (1963–f), also O. W. Ferguson, *Jonathan Swift and Ireland* (Urbana Ill. 1962) and L. A. Landa, *Swift and the Church of Ireland* (1954); M. R. O'Connell, *Irish politics and social conflict in the age of the American Revolution*,

(Philadelphia 1965); H. Butterfield, *George III, Lord North and the People* (1949); M. J. Craig, *The Volunteer Earl* (1948); T. H. Mahony, *Edmund Burke and Ireland* (Oxford 1960); R. Jacob, *The rise of the United Irishmen, 1791–4* (1937); R. R. Madden, *The United Irishmen, their lives and times*, 7 vols (1842–6), 4 vols (1857–60); H. M. Hyde, *The rise of Castlereagh* (1033); T. Pakenham, *The year of liberty: the great Irish rebellion of 1798* (1969). For the Irish parliament there is E. and A. G. Porritt, *The unreformed house of commons*, vol II (1903); E. M. Johnston, *Great Britain and Ireland* (1963); G. C. Bolton, *Passing of the Irish Act of Union* (1966) and also *The Parliamentary Register: or history of the proceedings and debates of the House of Commons of Ireland*, 15 vols (Dublin 1784–95); and T. Caldwell, *Debates relative to the affairs of Ireland in 1763 and 1764* (1766). For public opinion and the press see: R. B. McDowell, *Irish Public Opinion, 1750–1800* (1944); R. Munter, *The history of the Irish newspaper, 1685–1760* (Cambridge 1967); and B. Inglis, *The Freedom of the Press in Ireland 1784–1841* (1954).

(b) *Economic and social*. L. M. Cullen, *Anglo-Irish Trade, 1660–1800* (Manchester 1968), *An Economic history of Ireland since 1660* (1972) and *Life in Ireland* (1968); L. W. Hanson, *Contemporary printed sources for British and Irish economic history, 1701–1750*, (Cambridge 1963); G. N. Clark, *Guide to English commercial statistics, 1696–1782* (1938); T. J. Kiernan, *The financial administration of Ireland to 1817* (1930); J. O'Donovan, *The economic history of livestock in Ireland* (Cork 1940), C. Gill, *Rise of the Irish linen industry* (Oxford 1925, 1964); P. Lynch and J. Vaizey, *Guinness's Brewery in the Irish economy* (1960); F. G. Hall, *History of the Bank of Ireland, 1783–1946* (Dublin 1949), F. W. Fetter, *The Irish pound* (London 1955); W. A. McCutcheon, *The canals of the North of Ireland* (1965), V. T. H. and D. R. Delany, *The canals of the south of Ireland* (Newton Abbot 1966). K. H. Connell, *The population of*

Ireland, 1750–1845 (1950) and *Irish Peasant Society* (Oxford 1968); R. J. Dickson, *Ulster emigration to colonial America* (1966), J. C. O'Callaghan, *History of the Irish Brigades in the service of France* (Glasgow 1870). C. Maxwell, *Country and town in Ireland under the Georges* (1940, 1949) and *Dublin under the Georges, 1714–1830* (1956 edition), also *A history of Trinity College, Dublin* (Dublin 1946); J. J. Auchmuty, *Irish education, an historical survey* (Dublin 1937): M. Craig, *Dublin, 1660–1860* (1952), D. Guinness and W. Ryan, *Irish houses and castles* (1971); Georgian Society, *Records of eighteenth-century domestic architecture and decoration in Ireland,* 5 vols (Dublin 1909–13). D. Corkery, *The hidden Ireland* (Dublin 1925) should be studied in conjunction with L. M. Cullen's article in *Studia Hibernica* (1969) *q.v. infra*; M. Hurst, *Maria Edgeworth and the public scene: intellect, fine feeling and landlordism in the age of reform* (1969). T. W. Freeman, *Pre-famine Ireland: a study in historical geography* (1957).

(c) *Ecclesiastical.* There are few reliable secondary authorities. For a general survey see W. D. Killen, *Ecclesiastical history of Ireland,* 2 vols (1875) which has a slight Presbyterian bias. For the Catholic Church there is no comprehensive history but important work in this field has been published in pamphlets and articles by M. Wall, *q.v. infra*. There is also J. Brady and P. J. Corish, *The Church under the Penal Code* and its conjoint publication C. Giblin, *Irish Exiles in Catholic Europe* (Dublin 1971); interesting documentary material is available in J. Brady, *Catholics and Catholicism in the eighteenth-century press,* (Maynooth 1965). The standard Presbyterian history is J. S. Reid, ed. W. D. Killen, *History of the Presbyterian Church in Ireland,* 3 vols (Belfast 1867) which has a slight but not undue bias and a good survey is J. M. Barkley, *A short history of the Presbyterian church in Ireland* (Belfast 1959); an important work is J. C. Beckett's *Protestant dissent in Ireland, 1689–1780* (1948). The standard history of the Church of Ireland is

W. A. Philips ed., *History of the Church of Ireland,* 3 vols (Oxford 1933–4), it is biased but less so than J. T. Ball, *The reformed Church of Ireland, 1537–1886* (1886); a conscientious eighteenth-century clergyman is portrayed in S. Burdy, *The life of the late Philip Skelton,* (1792). For other denominations there is C. H. Crookshank, *History of Methodism in Ireland,* 3 vols (Belfast 1885–8); T. Wight and J. Rutty, *Rise and progress of the people called the Quakers in Ireland* (4th ed. 1811); A. Carré, *L'influence des Huguenots français en Irlande* (Paris 1937) which is also useful for social and economic history; and B. Shillman, *Short history of the Jews in Ireland,* (Dublin 1945).

3. Pamphlets. An important series of pamphlets is published by the Dublin Historical Association and includes, J. G. Simms, *The Jacobite Parliament of 1689* (1966) and *The Treaty of Limerick* (1961, 1965); M. Wall, *The Penal Laws, 1691–1760* (1961), J. L. McCracken, *The Irish Parliament in the eighteenth century* (1971). Another series, *Insights into Irish history,* is published by Gill & Macmillan on various social and economic topics, of particular relevance are L. M. Cullen, *Merchants, Ships and Trade, 1660–1830* (1971) and W. H. Crawford, *Domestic Industry in Ireland* (1971).

4. Articles in learned periodicals. The leading journal in this field is *Irish Historical Studies (IHS.)* and the following articles are of particular interest: J. G. Simms, 'The bishops' banishment act of 1697' (1970–1) and 'The making of a penal law, 1703–4' (1960); J. C. Beckett, 'William King's administration of the diocese of Derry, 1691–1703' (1944–5), 'The government of the Church of Ireland under William III and Anne' (1940–1), and 'Anglo-Irish constitutional relations in the later eighteenth century' (1964–5); J. L. McCracken, 'Irish parliamentary elections, 1727–68' (1947) and 'The conflict between the Irish administration and parliament' (1942–3); A. P. W. Malcomson, 'Election politics in the borough of Antrim,

1750–1800, (1970); P. Jupp, 'County Down elections, 1783–1831' (1972); D. Large ed. 'The Irish house of commons in 1769' (1958) – see *infra PRIA*, and 'The wealth of the greater Irish landowners, 1750–1815' (1966); L. M. Cullen, 'The value of contemporary printed sources for Irish economic history in the eighteenth century' (1964); M. MacGechin (Mrs Wall), 'The Catholics of the town and the quarterage dispute in eighteenth-century Ireland' (1952); T. M. O'Connor, 'The embargo on Irish provisions, 1776–9' (1940); J. J. Monaghan, 'The rise and fall of the Belfast cotton industry' (1942); E. R. R. Green, 'The Scotch-Irish and the coming of the Revolution in North Carolina' (1950); E. M. Johnston, 'The career and correspondence of Thomas Allan, *c.* 1725–98' (1957); J. E. Tyler 'A letter from the Marquess of Rockingham to Sir William Mayne on the proposed absentee tax of 1773' (1952–3); R. B. McDowell, 'The personnel of the Dublin Society of United Irishmen, 1791–4' (1940), 'The United Irish plans of parliamentary reform 1793' (1942), 'The Fitzwilliam episode' (1966–7) and 'The Irish courts of law 1801–1914' (1956–7) gives some information about the eighteenth century and a considerable amount of biographical detail.

Proceedings of the Royal Irish Academy. (PRIA). The following four papers give biographical details of members of the Irish parliament: M. Bodkin (ed.) 'Notes on the Irish parliament in 1773' (1942); G. O. Sayles (ed.), 'Contemporary sketches of members of the Irish Parliament in 1782' (1954); E. M. Johnston (ed.), 'Members of the Irish Parliament, 1784–7' (1971) and 'The Irish house of commons in 1791' (1957); (similar to these lists but published separately is W. Hunt (ed.), *The Irish parliament in 1775* (1907)). See also L. M. Cullen, 'The smuggling trade in Ireland in the eighteenth century' (1969) and A. P. W. Malcomson, 'John Foster and the Speakership of the Irish house of commons' (1972).

Studia Hibernica. L. M. Cullen, 'The Hidden Ireland: re-assessment of a concept' (1969) R. A. Butlin, 'Agriculture in County Dublin in the late eighteenth century' (1969).

English Historical Review (EHR). F. G. James, 'The Irish lobby in the early eighteenth century' (1966); C. L. Falkiner (ed.), 'Correspondence of Archbishop Stone and the Duke of Newcastle' (1905); J. A. Alger, 'An Irish Absentee and his tenants, 1768–92' (1895).

Past and Present. L. M. Cullen, 'Irish history without the potato' (1968).

Economic History Review. The following articles comment on K. H. Connell's important study.

The population of Ireland, 1750–1845 (1950): M. Drake, 'Marriage and Population Growth in Ireland, 1750–1845' (1963–4); J. Lee, 'Marriage and Population in Pre-famine Ireland' (1968); G. S. L. Tucker, 'Irish fertility ratios before the famine' (1970).

Transactions of the Royal Historical Society. L. M. Cullen, 'Problems in the interpretation and revision of eighteenth-century Irish economic history' (5th series, 1967).

American Philosophical Society. C. A. Edie, 'The Irish cattle bills – a study in Restoration politics' (1970).

Irish Sword. J. G. Simms, 'Eye-witnesses of the Boyne' (1963) and 'The siege of Derry' (1964).

Historical Studies. Papers read before the biennial Irish conference of historians are published in book form under this title, see particularly: J. G. Simms, 'The Irish parliament in 1713' (vol 4, 1963); M. Wall, 'The United Irish Movement' (vol 5, 1965); and J. A. Murphy, 'The support of the Catholic clergy in Ireland, 1750–1850' (vol 5, 1965).

Topic 13, a Journal of the Liberal Arts (Washington & Jefferson College, Pa. 1967) contains a number of studies in Irish history including L. M. Cullen, 'The re-interpretation of Irish economic history'.

References

THERE are few, if any, books listed in the bibliography which have not made some contribution to this study. Nevertheless, looking through my footnotes I am conscious of the particular debt which I owe to the studies of J. G. Simms, Maureen Wall, P. J. Corish, L. M. Cullen, Constantia Maxwell and Anthony Malcomson.

Virtually all of the quotations are from contemporary sources. Many of the official papers have been printed by H.M.S.O. including the *Calendars of Home Office Papers, 1760–76, Irish Official Papers in Great Britain* (P.R.O.N.I. 1973) and the various volumes of the *Historical Manuscripts Commission* W. E. H. Lecky, *History of Ireland in the eighteenth century* is still the most important secondary source and both Lecky and J. A. Froude, *The English in Ireland in the eighteenth century*, print large extracts from original documents usually state papers. For technical detail *English Historical Documents*, Grant Robertson; *Select Cases, Statutes and Documents* and Costain & Watson, *The law and working of the constitution* were useful. Printed memoirs and correspondence such as archbishop Boulter's *Letters*, Grattan's *Life*, Tone's *Autobiography* and Mrs Delany's *Correspondence* provided much political and social information. Extensive use was also made of Arthur Young's *Tour* and John Wesley's *Journal*.

Despite a policy of using sources already in print and reasonably available there remained a hard core of source material still in manuscript. The most important of these collections were the Newcastle MSS in the British Museum, used in conjunction with *The correspondence of archbishop Stone with the duke of Newcastle* printed in EHR 1905, the Devonshire MSS at Chatsworth and the Shannon MSS at Castlemartyr. As always the State Papers in the P.R.O. proved indispensable.

Index